HIGH SCHOOL
TALKSHEETS
ON THE NEW TESTAMENT
FOR AGES 14-18

EPIC BIBLE STORIES

52 READY-TO-USE DISCUSSIONS

DAVID LYNN

ZONDERVAN®

ZONDERVAN.com/
AUTHORTRACKER
follow your favorite authors

youth specialties

YOUTH SPECIALTIES

High School TalkSheets on the New Testament: 52 Ready-to-Use Discussions
Copyright 2009 by David Lynn

Youth Specialties resources, 1890 Cordell Ct. Ste. 105, El Cajon, CA 92020 are published by Zondervan, 5300 Patterson Ave. SE, Grand Rapids, MI 49530.

ISBN 978-0-310-66871-8

Cover design by David Conn
Interior design by Brandi Etheredge Design

Printed in the United States of America

22 • 20 19 18 17 16 15 14 13 12 11 10 9 8

For Amy:
Blessing #1

CONTENTS

THE HOWS AND WHATS
OF TALKSHEETS

about opinions, learn about themselves, and grow in their faith.

IMPORTANT GUIDING PRINCIPLES BEFORE USING NEW TESTAMENT TALKSHEETS

Let's begin by agreeing on two primary principles: (1) Faith is essentially caught, not taught, and (2) The Holy Spirit alone works best to establish faith within someone's life, changing someone from a knower to a believer and a church attendee to a lifelong follower of Jesus. If we can agree on these first principles, then it is easier to explain how NEW TESTAMENT TalkSheets is designed. It is not so much a teaching tool as a tool designed to engage real faith connections and encourage faith vocabulary in the lives of young people.

You are holding a very valuable book! No, it won't make you a genius or millionaire. But it does contain 52 instant discussions for high school youth. Inside you'll find reproducible NEW TESTAMENT TalkSheets that cover 52 stories from the birth of Jesus to the end of the book of Acts; plus simple, step-by-step instructions on how to use them. All you need is this book, a few copies of the handouts, and some young people (and maybe a snack or two). You're on your way to touching on some serious issues in young people's lives today.

These NEW TESTAMENT TalkSheets are user-friendly and very flexible. They can be used in a youth group meeting, a Sunday school class, or a Bible study group. You can adapt them for either large or small groups. And, they can be covered in only 20 minutes or explored more intensively in two hours.

You can build an entire youth group meeting around a single NEW TESTAMENT TalkSheet, or you can use NEW TESTAMENT TalkSheets to supplement other materials and resources you might be using. These are tools for you—how you use them is your choice.

High School NEW TESTAMENT TalkSheets is not your average curriculum or workbook. This collection of discussions will get your young people involved and excited about talking through important issues. The NEW TESTAMENT TalkSheets deal with epic stories and include interesting activities, challenging questions, and eye-catching graphics. They will challenge your young people to think

So many church attendees do not know how to articulate their faith, nor do they often see real, vital connections for their faith outside of the church building. NEW TESTAMENT TalkSheets exercises are designed to help young people make real life connections between what they believe and their day-to-day lives, as well as develop a living faith vocabulary, as opposed to a church vocabulary used only in the God house to please adults and religious leaders. For faith to grow with us in ways that last a lifetime, all of us need to discover faith's vital connection in our day-to-day lives. We need to see where Jesus in our lives engages the real world we live in. And we need to have an ability to express this connection, or have a "vocabulary of faith" that grows with us and goes with us, rather than merely a religious Christian-ese we speak in religious settings and on certain occasions.

These NEW TESTAMENT TalkSheets exercises are aimed at engaging young people in real conversations where belief can be discovered, Christian words and notions can be unpacked, and faith can be connected with and expressed. In such settings the earliest Christians explored and expressed their faith. Our Lord Jesus used fishing with fishermen to connect his first followers with what he was doing, using words and images that were familiar to them. Creating settings where young people can talk about faith develops a faith vocabulary and deepens faith by connecting it to relevant life experiences.

NEW TESTAMENT TALKSHEETS AS AN ENGAGING TOOL RATHER THAN A TEACHING TOOL

We have often made a very fundamental mistake in how we assist young people in their faith development. We have hammered down on the obvious answers to questions that the young people are often not even asking. What you wind up with are young people who can answer the question "correctly" but don't see why the answer is relevant to their daily lives.

Take, for example, the primary question of faith: Who is your Lord and Savior? The right answer is "Jesus Christ is my Lord and Savior." I have heard young people answer this question correctly for many years. But when it comes to real life, I have also witnessed many young people get stumped on a valid understanding as to what "Lord" means in a culture where all people are their own sources of truth or as to why they need to be saved when all people are "basically okay." We often make the mistake of assuming that good information is enough. But the information needs to possess something vital for youth to attach to, and if the questions are not there, the information may not seem relevant.

When we teach young people answers to questions they are not asking, nor even know that they need to ask, we are leaving them with answers that don't fit and faith that will not stand up under pressure. This is why we believe that young people need to understand the tensions of life from which questions arise and struggle with how they answer those questions daily in their lives before they hear how God has addressed those questions in the person of Jesus Christ. Then we can ask, "If this is how life is, then who is YOUR Lord and Savior?"

By engaging young people inwardly and INNER-gizing young people into a real dialogue about their life, perceptions, and faith, we can make pathways where we can partner with them as they grow in their discipleship.

A COMMON PITFALL TO AVOID

Faith development is often a stepped process. Some things need to be set in place before other things can be embraced. We might say that a person moves from A to B before moving on to C and eventually arriving at D. A mistake many leaders may make is that the movement from A to D looks simple to them, and they are impatient for those they are working with to make that developmental leap. Good Christian leadership understands that we are often guides for encounters on the roadside as people make their way in following the Master.

A pitfall that is common in Christian leadership is to invite people to make a leap in faith development they're unable to sustain. Often young believers make a substitutional leap of faith and jump from A to D based on what the leader believes. People are very willing to do this because they might trust their leaders or might be afraid to express real doubts in an unsafe environment. They might also think it's a lack on their part to move so slowly in faith, which can make them feel guilty. There's also performance anxiety in our faith settings that can cause people to take on language that fits the situation but is essentially not a part of their day-to-day lives.

I have witnessed these conditions, where real faith is not deep enough to sustain the pressures of real life and substitutional faith is worn like a garment in the God house. Such followers who attend gatherings but cannot pray for themselves hold a secret sense of doubt and guilt and often defer to the religious leadership on all matters of faith.

Jesus spoke of such followers, who are like shallow soil on which the seed falls.

Essentially there are three roles a discussion leader can fulfill: An Instrument, a Thorn, or a Stage Director: (1) An Instrument can be a force in the hand of the Holy Spirit that works in the process of faith-building in the life of young disciples; (2) As a Thorn the leader can become an irritant in the life of disciples that alienates them from the faith community by creating an unsafe faith environment with unrealistic expectations and impatient discipleship methods; (3) A Stage Director leader is one who inoculates young people against catching real faith by creating an environment that encourages satisfying an expectation by taking on a mask of believing and a language of the church. This effactully insulates them from embracing real, vital faith expressed in a living language. As you can see, only one role serves well in the life of young followers, and that is the role of an Instrument.

NEW TESTAMENT TALKSHEETS HELPS US BE GOOD STEWARDS OF A SACRED PROCESS

But if we understand deep, rich soil may take time and much mulching if a seed is to take root, then we can as leaders trust that faith is not about ourselves achieving something in the life of a person, but about the Holy Spirit shaping a life into a follower. We can become stewards of a most sacred process. Young people can pick up useless notions of faith and life on their way to discovering real faith that rumbles deep with a vital discipleship. Patient and loving mentoring is needed if these useless notions are to be replaced with life-giving awareness in a living, vital faith in Jesus.

Remember that Thomas did not at first believe that Jesus was resurrected even though the other disciples expressed to him what they had witnessed. It is a great testimony of those early followers of Jesus that Thomas was still with them "in their midst" a week later when Jesus showed up and confirmed himself to Thomas. It is important to create a safe environment where young people can explore their faith and express themselves without the expectation of correct performance or the need to make the developmental leap that they are not ready to sustain as a disciple until, for them, Jesus shows up.

LEADING A NEW TESTAMENT TALKSHEET DISCUSSION

NEW TESTAMENT TalkSheets can be used as a curriculum for your youth group, but they are designed to be springboards for discussion. They encourage your young people to take part and interact with each other while talking about real life issues. And hopefully they'll do some serious thinking, discover new ideas for themselves, defend their points of view, and make decisions.

Youth today face a world of moral confusion. Youth leaders must teach the church's beliefs and values—and also help young people make the right choices in a world full of options. Teenagers are bombarded with the voices of society and the media—most of which drown out what they hear from the church.

A NEW TESTAMENT TalkSheet discussion works for this very reason. While dealing with the questions and activities on the NEW TESTAMENT TalkSheet, your young people will think carefully about issues, compare their beliefs and values with others, and make their own choices. NEW TESTAMENT TalkSheets will challenge your group to explain and rework their ideas in a Christian atmosphere of acceptance, support, and growth.

The most common fear of high school youth group leaders is, "What will I do if the young people in my group just sit there and don't say anything?" Well, when young people don't have anything to say, it's because they haven't had a chance or time to get their thoughts organized! Most young people haven't developed the ability to think on their feet. Since many are afraid they might sound stupid, they don't know how to voice their ideas and opinions.

The solution? NEW TESTAMENT TalkSheets let your youth deal with the issues in a challenging, non-threatening way before the actual discussion begins. They'll have time to organize their thoughts, write them down, and ease their fears about participating. They may even look forward to sharing their answers! Most importantly, they'll want to find out what others say and open up to talk through the topics.

If you're still a little leery about the success of a real discussion among your youth, that's okay!

YOUR ROLE AS THE LEADER

The best discussions don't happen by accident. They require careful preparation and a sensitive leader. Don't worry if you aren't experienced or don't have hours to prepare. NEW TESTAMENT TalkSheets are designed to help even the novice leader! The more NEW TESTAMENT TalkSheet discussions you lead, the easier it becomes. Keep the following tips in mind when using the NEW TESTAMENT TalkSheets as you get your young people talking.

BE CHOOSY

Each NEW TESTAMENT TalkSheet deals with a different story. Under the title of each of the NEW TESTAMENT TalkSheets is a simple subtitle heading that expresses the theme of the TalkSheet. Choose a NEW TESTAMENT TalkSheet based on the needs and the maturity level of your group. Don't feel obligated to use the NEW TESTAMENT TalkSheets in the order they appear in this book. Use your best judgment and mix them up however you want— they're tools for you!

MAKE COPIES

Young people will need their own copy of the TalkSheet. Only make copies of the youth side of the TalkSheet! The material on the reverse side (the leader's guide) is just for you. You're able to make copies for your group because we have given you permission to do so. U.S. copyright laws have not changed, and it is still mandatory to request permission from a publisher before making copies of other published material. It is against the law not to do so. However, permission is given for you to make copies of this material for your group only, not for every youth group in your state. Thank you for cooperating.

TRY IT YOURSELF

Once you have chosen a NEW TESTAMENT TalkSheet for your group, answer the questions and do the activities yourself. Imagine your young people's reactions to the NEW TESTAMENT TalkSheet. This will help you prepare for the discussion and understand what you are asking them to do. Plus, you'll have some time to think of other appropriate questions, activities, and Bible verses.

GET SOME INSIGHT

On each leader's guide page, you'll find numerous tips and ideas for getting the most out of your discussion. You may want to add some of your own thoughts or ideas in the margins.

INTRODUCE THE TOPIC

You may introduce the topic before you pass out the NEW TESTAMENT TalkSheets to your group, and then allow the topic to develop as you use the material. We have a simple format on the leader's guide that can help your introduction. First, there is the "Read Out Loud" section. Simply read the paragraph or two out loud, then ask a young person to read the story from the Bible. After the story is read, you can use the question in the "Ask" section to get the group primed for a discussion of the story.

NEW TESTAMENT TalkSheets work best with a strong concluding presentation rather than a strong teaching time prior to using the Talksheet. You can use the "Close" section to help guide your closing presentation. Depending on your group, keep your introduction short and to the point. Be careful not to over-introduce the topic, sound preachy, or resolve the issue before you've started. Your goal is to spark their interest and leave plenty of room for discussion, allowing the material to introduce the topic.

Pass out the NEW TESTAMENT TalkSheet and be sure that everyone has a pencil or pen. Now you're on your way! The following are excellent methods you can use to introduce any topic in this book—

- Show a related short film or video.
- Read a passage from a book or magazine that relates to the subject.
- Play a popular CD that deals with the topic.
- Perform a short skit or dramatic presentation.
- Play a simulation game or role-play, setting up the topic.
- Present current statistics or survey results, or read a current newspaper article that provides recent information about the topic.
- Use an icebreaker or other crowd game, getting into the topic in a humorous way.
- Use posters, videos, or any other visuals to help focus attention on the topic.

There are endless possibilities for an intro—you're limited only by your own creativity! Keep in mind that a clear and simple introduction is a very important part of each session.

SET BOUNDARIES
It'll be helpful to set a few ground rules before the discussion. Keep the rules to a minimum, of course, but let the youth know what's expected of them. Here are suggestions for some basic ground rules:
- What's said in this room stays in this room. Emphasize the importance of confidentiality.

Some young people will open up, some won't. Confidentiality is vital for a good discussion. If your youth can't keep the discussion in the room, then they won't open up.
- No put-downs. Mutual respect is important. If your young people disagree with some opinions, ask them to comment on the subject (but not on the other person).
- There's no such thing as a dumb question. Your group members must feel free to ask questions at any time. The best way to learn is to ask questions and get answers.
- No one is forced to talk. Let everyone know they have the right to pass or not answer any question.
- Only one person speaks at a time. This is a mutual respect issue. Everyone's opinion is worthwhile and deserves to be heard.

Communicate with your group that everyone needs to respect these boundaries. If you sense that your group members are attacking each other or getting a negative attitude during the discussion, do stop and deal with the problem before going on.

ALLOW ENOUGH TIME
Pass out copies of the NEW TESTAMENT TalkSheet to your young people after the introduction and make sure that each person has a pen or pencil and a Bible. There are usually five or six activities on each NEW TESTAMENT TalkSheet. If your time is limited, or if you are using only a part of the NEW TESTAMENT TalkSheet, tell the group to complete only the activities you assign.

Decide ahead of time whether or not you would like the young people to work on the NEW TESTAMENT TalkSheet individually or in groups.

Let them know how much time they have for completing the NEW TESTAMENT TalkSheet and let them know when there is a minute (or so) left. Go ahead and give them some extra time, and then start the discussion when everyone seems ready to go.

SET THE STAGE

Create a climate of acceptance. Most teenagers are afraid to voice their opinions because they don't want to be laughed at or look stupid in front of their peers. They want to feel safe if they're going to share their feelings and beliefs. Communicate that they can share their thoughts and ideas—even if they may be different or unpopular. If your young people get put-downs, criticism, laughter, or snide comments (even if their statements are opposed to the teachings of the Bible), it'll hurt the discussion.

Always phrase your questions—even those that are printed on the NEW TESTAMENT TalkSheets—so that you are asking for an opinion, not an answer. For example, if a question reads, "What should Bill have done in that situation?" the simple addition of the three words "do you think" makes the question less threatening and a matter of opinion, rather than a demand for the right answer. Your young people will relax when they feel more comfortable and confident. Plus, they'll know that you actually care about their opinions and they'll feel appreciated!

LEAD THE DISCUSSION

Discuss the NEW TESTAMENT TalkSheet with the group and encourage all your young people to participate. Communicate that it's important for them to respect each other's opinions and feelings! The more they contribute, the better the discussion will be.

If your youth group is big, you may divide it into smaller groups of six to 12. Each of these small groups should have a facilitator—either an adult leader or a youth member—to keep the discussion going. Remind the facilitators not to dominate. If the group looks to the facilitator for an answer, ask him or her to direct the questions or responses back to the group. Once the smaller groups have completed their discussions, combine them into one large group and ask the different groups to share their ideas.

You don't have to divide the groups up with every NEW TESTAMENT TalkSheet. For some discus-

sions, you may want to vary the group size and/or divide the meeting into groups of the same sex.

The discussion should target the questions and answers on the NEW TESTAMENT TalkSheet. Go through them one at a time and ask the young people to share their responses. Have them compare their answers and brainstorm new ones in addition to the ones they've written down. Encourage them to share their opinions and answers, but don't force those who are quiet.

AFFIRM ALL RESPONSES—RIGHT OR WRONG

Let your young people know that their comments and contributions are appreciated and important. This is especially true for those who rarely speak during group activities. Make a point of thanking them for joining in. This will be an incentive for them to participate further.

Remember that affirmation doesn't mean approval. Affirm even those comments that seem wrong to you. You'll show that everyone has a right to express their ideas—no matter how controversial they may be. If someone states an opinion that is off base, make a mental note of the comment. Then in your wrap-up, come back to the comment or present a different point of view in a positive way. But don't reprimand the person who voiced the comment.

DON'T BE THE AUTHORITATIVE ANSWER

Some young people think you have the right to answer to every question. They'll look to you for approval, even when they are answering another group member's question. If they start to focus on you for answers, redirect them toward the group by making a comment like, "Remember that you're talking to everyone, not just me."

Your goal as the facilitator is to keep the discussion alive and kicking. It's important that your young people think of you as a member of the group—on their level. The less authoritative you are, the more value your own opinions will have. If your young people view you as a peer, they will listen to your comments. You have a tremendous responsibility to be, with sincerity, their trusted friend.

LISTEN TO EACH PERSON
God gave you one mouth and two ears. Good discussion leaders know how to listen. Although it's tempting at times, don't monopolize the discussion. Encourage others to talk first—then express your opinions during your wrap-up.

DON'T FORCE IT
Encourage all your young people to talk, but don't make them comment. Each member has the right to pass. If you feel that the discussion isn't going well, go on to the next question or restate the question to keep them moving.

DON'T TAKE SIDES
You'll probably have different opinions expressed in the group from time to time. Be extra careful not to take one side or another. Encourage both sides to think through their positions—ask questions to get them deeper. If everyone agrees on an issue, you can play devil's advocate with tough questions and stretch their thinking. Remain neutral—your point of view is your own, not that of the group.

DON'T LET ANYONE (INCLUDING YOU) TAKE OVER
Nearly every youth group has one person who likes to talk and is perfectly willing to express an opinion on any subject. Try to encourage equal participation from all the young people.

SET UP FOR THE TALK
Make sure that the seating arrangement is inclusive and encourages a comfortable, safe atmosphere for discussion. Theater-style seating (in rows) isn't discussion-friendly. Instead, arrange the chairs in a circle or semicircle (or sit on the floor with pillows).

LET THEM LAUGH!
Discussions can be fun! Most of the NEW TESTAMENT TalkSheets include questions that'll make them laugh and get them thinking, too.

LET THEM BE SILENT
Silence can be scary for discussion leaders! Some react by trying to fill the silence with a question or comment. The following suggestions may help you to handle silence more effectively:

- Be comfortable with silence. Wait it out for 30 seconds or so to respond. You may want to restate the question to give your young people a gentle nudge.
- Talk about the silence with the group. What does the silence mean? Do they really not have any comments? Maybe they're confused or embarrassed or don't want to share.
- Answer the silence with questions or comments like, "I know this is challenging to think about…" or "It's scary to be the first to talk." If you acknowledge the silence, it may break the ice.
- Ask a different question that may be easier to handle or that will clarify the one already posed. But don't do this too quickly without giving them time to think the first one through.

KEEP IT UNDER CONTROL
Monitor the discussion. Be aware if the discussion is going in a certain direction or off track. This can happen fast, especially if the young people disagree or things get heated. Mediate wisely and set the tone that you want. If your group gets bored with an issue, get them back on track. Let the discussion unfold, but be sensitive to your group and who is or is not getting involved.

If a young person brings up a side issue that's interesting, decide whether or not to pursue it. If discussion is going well and the issue is worth discussion, let them talk it through. But, if things get way off track, say something like, "Let's come back to that subject later if we have time. Right now, let's finish our discussion on…"

BE CREATIVE AND FLEXIBLE

You don't have to follow the order of the questions on the NEW TESTAMENT TalkSheet. Follow your own creative instinct. If you find other ways to use the NEW TESTAMENT TalkSheets, use them! Go ahead and add other questions or Bible references.

Don't feel pressured to spend time on every single activity. If you're short on time, you can skip some items. Stick with the questions that are the most interesting to the group.

SET YOUR GOALS

NEW TESTAMENT TalkSheets are designed to move along toward a goal, but you need to identify your goal in advance. What would you like your young people to learn? What truth should they discover? What is the goal of the session? If you don't know where you're going, it's doubtful you will get there. As stated earlier, there is a theme for each of the NEW TESTAMENT TalkSheets. You will find this theme in smaller type in the heading of each of the TalkSheet titles.

BE THERE FOR YOUR YOUNG PEOPLE

Some young people may want to talk more with you (you got 'em thinking!). Let them know that you can talk one-on-one with them afterward.

Communicate to the young people that they can feel free to talk with you about anything with confidentiality. Let them know you're there for them with support and concern, even after the NEW TESTAMENT TalkSheet discussion has been completed.

CLOSE THE DISCUSSION

There is a "Close" section at the end of each of the leader guides with a paragraph or two of closing comments. Present a challenge to the group by asking yourself, "What do I want the young people to remember most from this discussion?" There's your wrap up!

Sometimes you won't need a wrap-up. You may want to leave the issue hanging and discuss it in another meeting. That way, your group can think about it more and you can nail down the final ideas later.

A FINAL WORD TO THE WISE— THAT'S YOU!

Some of these NEW TESTAMENT TalkSheets deal with topics that may be sensitive or controversial for your young people. You're encouraging discussion and inviting your young people to express their opinions. As a result, parents or others in your church may criticize you—they may not see the importance of such discussions. Use your best judgment. If you suspect that a particular NEW TESTAMENT TalkSheet will cause problems, you may not want to use it. Or you may want to tweak a particular NEW TESTAMENT TalkSheet and only cover some of the questions. Either way, the potential bad could outweigh the good—better safe than sorry. To avoid any misunderstanding, you may want to give the parents or senior pastor (or whomever else you are accountable to) copies of the NEW TESTAMENT TalkSheet before you use it. Let them know the discussion you would like to have and the goal you are hoping to accomplish. Challenge your young people to take their NEW TESTAMENT TalkSheet home to talk about it with their parents. How would their parents, as young people, have answered the questions? Your young people may find that their parents understand them better than they thought. Also, encourage them to think of other Bible verses or ways that the NEW TESTAMENT TalkSheet applies to their lives.

A SAVIOR GETS A NAME

Jesus' name tells us what we celebrate at Christmas

1. I sense God being with me . . .

   ☐ Quite often
   ☐ Sometimes
   ☐ Hardly ever
   ☐ Never

2. If you were to write a Christmas song about Joseph, what would be the theme?

3. The angel told Joseph to give the baby the "name Jesus, because he will save his people from their sins" (Matthew 1:21). **A (agree)** or **D (disagree)** with the following statements about sin.

   ___ People like to make sin a good thing—like calling Las Vegas "Sin City."
   ___ Sinful things are used to advertise products.
   ___ You don't hear much about sin today except in church.
   ___ Movies about sinful things are never popular.
   ___ Christians can keep sinning as long as they ask for forgiveness.
   ___ People are less tempted today to sin than they were during the time of Jesus' earthly ministry.
   ___ Some sins aren't that bad—like "little white lies."

4. The name *Jesus* is deeply connected to the idea of saving and salvation from sin. Who needs to be saved?

   • Old people trying to get into heaven
   • Only those who think they need to be saved
   • People who still believe in sin
   • Those who are separated from God
   • Atheists
   • Those who don't go to church
   • Me

5. Jesus could not have been God and a man at the same time.

   TRUE or FALSE?

6. Read Isaiah 9:6, which lists four other names for Jesus. Circle the one name that describes a characteristic of Jesus that you need right now —

   Wonderful Counselor   *Mighty God*   *Everlasting Father*   *Prince of Peace*

*For to us a child is born, to us a son is given, and the government will be on his shoulders.
And he will be called Wonderful Counselor, Mighty God, Everlasting Father, Prince of Peace. (Isaiah 9:6)*

READ OUT LOUD

Joseph and Mary were "pledged" to marry—a getting-to-know-each-other period that connected them mentally, spiritually, and emotionally, ending with the act of marriage and physical intimacy. Stronger than today's engagement, this pledge could only be ended by divorce. Joseph and Mary were getting to know each other well before they had sex in marriage. This is where today's story begins. Read Matthew 1:18-25.

ASK

What do you have to do to get one of your parents to use your full name?

DISCUSS, BY THE NUMBERS

1. One of the names of Jesus, Immanuel, means "God with us." Let your group members share the answers they checked off. It's easy for your group members to give you the Sunday school answer. This can be avoided by giving a real answer—share those times when you haven't sensed God's presence in your life. Say, "God is present in all the situations we face every day from lunch in the cafeteria to worship at church. Our job is to train ourselves to sense God's presence in the ordinary situations of life."

2. Joseph consistently did what God asked of him, without questioning or grumbling. And yet there are no Christmas songs about Joseph! Joseph is the kind of person we want to become—like Christ in all he did.

3. See commentary in bold after each statement. This item looks at sin today. Remember, God the Father told Joseph to give Jesus his name because "he will save his people from their sins."

   - People like to make sin a good thing—like calling Las Vegas "Sin City." **Today, sin is celebrated and glorified.**
   - Sinful things are used to advertise products. **Ask your group members why.**

- You don't hear much about sin today except in church. **Ask, "What do you hear about sin in church? How is that different than what the world says about sin?"**
- Movies about sinful things are never popular. **Point out that the consequences of sin are rarely seen in the movies.**
- Christians can keep sinning as long as they ask for forgiveness. **A great faith-conversation starter.**
- People are less tempted today to sin than they were during the time of Jesus' earthly ministry. **No. People have always been tempted to sin.**
- Some sins aren't that bad—like "little white lies." **In the eyes of God, sin is sin. However, our culture wants to diminish the nature of sin.**

4. Ask, "Do people need to be saved from their sins?" Then, "Why or why not?"

5. To save us from our sins, Jesus had to be fully human (to take our sins upon himself) and fully God (to rise again from death). Called the hypostatic union, this mystery of the God-man is discussed in 1 Timothy 3:16.

6. Read Isaiah 9:6 out loud. Ask why your group members circled the names that they did.

THE CLOSE

The Christmas season is that time of year that we celebrate "Immanuel." The Christmas season is also a time to reflect on what Christ has done for us as the God-Man. And finally, the Christmas season is that time of year when we can remember why Jesus is our Savior and Lord. This year let's reach beyond shopping and decorating and remember the reason for the season. Jesus' name tells us what we celebrate at Christmas.

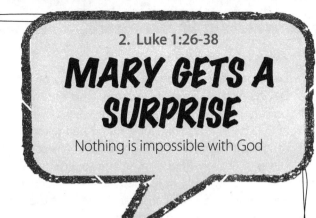

2. Luke 1:26-38

MARY GETS A SURPRISE

Nothing is impossible with God

1. The angel told Mary she was really special and that God was with her.

How are you special to the Lord?

How do you want the Lord to be with you this Christmas season?

What would you like the Lord to do through you this next year?

2. Finish these two sentences:

• I am afraid of God when—

• God is pleased with me because—

3. I have seen God do an impossible thing in my life or someone else's life. (Circle one)

Yes   **No**   **Maybe So**

4. On the line scale below, indicate with an X your degree of willingness to serve God.

■□□□□□□□□□□□□□□□□□□□□□□□□□□□□□□□□□□□□□□■

I am totally willing to
do anything that
God asks of me.

I am totally unwilling
to do anything that
God asks of me.

5. God surprised Mary with the miracle of Jesus. God wants to surprise you. What impossible thing needs to happen in your life?

2. MARY GETS A SURPRISE—Nothing is impossible with God (Luke 1:26-38)

READ OUT LOUD

Both Mary and Joseph were descendants of King David's family. Living in Nazareth, a small town in Galilee, they were away from the envy of Herod, who lived in Jerusalem. King Herod had taken the throne that rightfully belonged to the heirs of King David. Mary, pledged in marriage to Joseph, was not expecting what happened next. Her pledge to Joseph was more than an arrangement like today's engagement. A marriage pledge was a time for a couple to get to know each other before sexual intimacy. The pledge could only be broken through divorce. Read today's story, found in Luke 1:26-38.

ASK

Who do you know who has accomplished the impossible?

DISCUSS, BY THE NUMBERS

1. Ask your group members to respond to each of the three questions. Use these questions as an opportunity to spark a faith conversation about the "specialness" of each of your group members to the Lord. As with Mary, God wants to be with each of your group members and do a great work in each of their lives.
2. Read Luke 1:30 out loud. Ask a group member or two to complete both sentence stems. Ask, "What do you do with your fears of God? Why are you glad that God is pleased with you?"

But the angel said to her, "Do not be afraid, Mary, you have found favor with God." (Luke 1:30)

3. God is in the "impossible" business. Talk about the different impossible things you have seen God do in your life or in the lives of those you know. Ask, "Why do you think God still does impossible things in the lives of believers? What impossible thing would you like God to do in your life?"
4. Mary was willing to allow God to do whatever God wanted in her life. Use this item to check your group members' willingness to allow God to work in their

lives. Read Luke 1:38 out loud after getting feedback regarding the line scale. Ask, "What is one thing that you hope Christ wants to do with your life?" and, "What is one thing that you hope Christ won't want to do with your life?"

"I am the Lord's servant," Mary answered. "May it be to me according to your word." Then the angel left her. (Luke 1:38)

5. Listen to each of your group members' answers. Let the group give each other feedback about their responses.

THE CLOSE

God is in the "impossible" business. We live in a world that is skeptical of the existence of a God who is intimately involved in our lives. We live in a world that says it is up to us to do the impossible. We live in a world where hard work and a little luck are supposed to make the impossible happen. But this is not reality. It is God who makes the impossible possible. It is God who is waiting for us to rely on him to do the impossible. It is God who wants us to pray for the impossible.

Challenge your group members to pray for God to do the impossible in their lives and to pray this prayer every day until they get an answer.

ab

1. **Finish this sentence:** The thing that sidetracks me the most at Christmas is —

2. **How do you think Caesar Augustus received Jesus? How about the manager of the inn? The residents of Bethlehem?**

JESUS IS BORN

What do people do with Jesus at Christmas?

3. **Do you think that each of these statements is T (true) or F (false)?**

___ Most people today ignore Jesus during the Christmas season.

___ People are too busy at the Christmas season with things other than Jesus.

___ Attending a church service helps me remember the reason for the season.

___ Decorating a Christmas tree ignores the true meaning of Christmas.

___ People who attend church only during Christmas (and maybe Easter) will still go to heaven.

___ We can receive the gift of Jesus every day of the year.

___ Nativity scenes in public places are good because they remind people of the true meaning of Christmas.

4. **Check your answer to each of the following questions.**

	REJECT	ACCEPT
What do your friends do with Jesus at Christmas?	☐	☐
What does your family do with Jesus at Christmas?	☐	☐
What does your congregation do with Jesus at Christmas?	☐	☐
What do your neighbors do with Jesus at Christmas?	☐	☐
What does your school/work do with Jesus at Christmas?	☐	☐

5. **How will you get yourself ready to celebrate the birth of Christ this Christmas?**

- I won't.
- I will attend a special church service.
- My family does special activities during the Christmas season.
- I will read my Bible and pray.
- I will listen to Christmas music.
- I will do a service project that helps the poor.
- I will watch Christmas movies.
- I will light the candles on an Advent wreath with my family.
- Other: _____

6. **When your friends ask you what you got for Christmas, how can you use this as an opportunity to talk with them about Christ?**

From *High School TalkSheets on the New Testament: 52 Ready-to-Use Discussions* by David Lynn. Permission to reproduce this page granted only for use in buyer's youth group. Copyright © 2009 David Lynn

READ OUT LOUD

Jesus was born into poverty. At the height of the violent Roman Empire, Jesus comes into this world in a town called Bethlehem just as the Old Testament predicted (Micah 5:2). Not born in a place of power or wealth, Jesus chose to identify with the impoverished and powerless. Our story picks up in Luke 2:1-7.

ASK

Do you rip open your Christmas gifts or slowly peel away the tape and paper?

DISCUSS, BY THE NUMBERS

1. Point out that we all can get sidetracked during the Christmas season. Create a list of completed sentences of reasons for getting sidetracked.

2. When Christ was born he was a subject of the Roman Empire. Caesar Augustus, the supreme dictator who ruled the Empire at the time, never knew about Jesus because he wasn't interested in a Savior and Lord. In fact, he thought that savior and lord were his roles. And what kind of treatment did the inn manager give Jesus and his parents? He banished them to the stable, where the animals were kept! Is that a suitable place in which to birth the Savior of the world? Finally, there are the residents of Bethlehem, who appear to have all but ignored the family of Jesus. Ask, "Why do you think Jesus allowed himself to be born in such humiliating circumstances?"

3. See commentary in bold after each statement.
   - Most people today ignore Jesus during the Christmas season. **Ask why. And talk about how we, as Christians, ignore Jesus during the Christmas season. Is this done on purpose?**
   - People are too busy at the Christmas season with things other than Jesus. **Make a list of what keeps people too busy.**
   - Attending a church service helps me remember the reason for the season. **Talk about what your church does during the Christmas season.**
   - Decorating a Christmas tree ignores the true meaning of Christmas. **Debate this one.**
   - People who attend church only during Christmas (and maybe Easter) will still go to heaven. **Talk about why church attendance has nothing to do with salvation. Also talk about the importance of church attendance and participation for Christian growth.**
   - We can receive the gift of Jesus every day of the year. **True, but only if we choose to.**
   - Nativity scenes in public places are good because they remind people of the true meaning of Christmas. **Debate the pros and cons of this.**

4. This item looks at what different groups of people do with Jesus during the Christmas season. Talk together about each of the groups of people—friends, family, congregation, neighbors, and those at school/work. The Christmas season can be an opportunity to talk about Christ with each of these groups of people. You don't have to leave Jesus in a manger at Christmas!

5. Use this item as an opportunity to talk about the best ways to celebrate the birth of Christ during the Christmas season.

6. Role play, if time permits, different situations that can happen at Christmas as opportunities to share Christ.

THE CLOSE

Christmas is a time in which we have a choice—a choice of what we will do with Jesus. Will we ignore him like the Roman leaders? Will we banish him to the back of our lives as the manager of the inn and the townspeople of Bethlehem did? Or will we celebrate his birth and lift him up as Savior and Lord?

1. Revelation 12:4 tells us that Satan wanted to get rid of Jesus before he was born. How do you think Satan wants to distract you from doing what God wants you to do?

RUNNING TO EGYPT

God uses circumstances to guide the direction of our lives

2. Check your response to each of the following statements.

	NONE OF THE TIME	HALF OF THE TIME	ALL OF THE TIME
My life is going in the right direction.	☐	☐	☐
I have a feel for what God wants me to do.	☐	☐	☐
God is actively working in my life.	☐	☐	☐
Jesus is real to me.	☐	☐	☐
God is using the circumstances in my life to mold me into the person he wants me to be.	☐	☐	☐

3. Joseph and Mary put their trust in God as they fled to Egypt—and God provided. How has your life worked out since you have put your trust in Christ?

4. Read the statement and decide if you A (agree) or D (disagree).

___ God uses circumstances in our lives to keep us humble.

___ Jesus' parents, Mary and Joseph, were humbled because there was no room at any of the inns in Bethlehem and then they had to run to Egypt.

___ It's easy for me to be humble.

___ Herod's humility helped him rule the Jews.

___ Arrogance will get you further in life than humility.

5. In today's story of Joseph, God did what he promised he would do. Why do you think you can count on God to do what he says he will do? What do you think God has promised you?

6. God spoke to Joseph in a dream. How does God speak to you?

READ OUT LOUD
King Herod, the local ruler who was placed in charge by the Roman Empire at the time of Jesus' birth, wanted to kill the baby Jesus. Herod, wanting to remove any competition for power, may have been aware of Jesus' ancestry. Both Mary and Joseph were from the line of King David, and thus Jesus would have a claim to Herod's throne. Read Matthew 2:13-23.

ASK
When you get lost do you ask for directions?

DISCUSS, BY THE NUMBERS
1. These two extremes are both dangerous. Satan would love it if we didn't believe in his existence, freeing him to do his evil without our interference, or if we believed that he has more power than he, in fact, does. Below, find some biblical perspective on Satan.
   - Satan waits for opportunities to attack believers. *Be alert and of sober mind. Your enemy the devil prowls around like a roaring lion looking for someone to devour. (1 Peter 5:8)*
   - Satan hopes to disgrace you. *He must also have a good reputation with outsiders, so that he will not fall into disgrace and into the devil's trap. (1 Timothy 3:7)*
   - Satan is trying to fool or trick you so, protect yourself. *Put on the full armor of God, so that you can take your stand against the devils' schemes. (Ephesians 6:11)*
   - Satan has no power to do anything in your life that can harm you without God's permission. *We know that anyone born of God does not continue to sin; the One who was born of God keeps them safe, and the evil one cannot harm them. (1 John 5:18)*
   - Satan hopes that your anger will get out of control so that he can influence you to sin. *"In your anger do not sin": Do not let the sun go down while you are still angry, and do not give the devil a foothold. (Ephesians 4:26-27)*
2. Herod wished to kill Jesus. The wise men gave expensive gifts to Jesus. This provided for Jesus' family while in Egypt. Herod's son, the cruel Archelaus, gave Joseph pause about going to Jerusalem. An angel directed him to Galilee, a safe place in which to raise Jesus. These circumstances guided the life of Joseph and fulfilled predictions made in the Old Testament about Jesus. God uses circumstances to guide the direction of our lives. Each of these statements gives you a chance to talk about God's guidance in your life and the lives of your young people. It could be helpful to share a story from your life regarding how God used your life circumstances to guide you in the right direction.
3. Have a discussion about times when you and your group members have put (and not put) your trust in Christ and the consequences of those decisions. It is just as important to talk about those life experiences in which you and your group members trusted in yourselves rather than Christ.
4. See commentary in bold after each statement.
   - God uses circumstances in our lives to keep us humble. **Yes. Ask for stories of how this has happened or tell a story from your life.**
   - Jesus' parents, Mary and Joseph, were humbled because there was no room at any of the inns in Bethlehem, and then they had to run to Egypt. **Yes, both experiences would have kept them relying on God.**
   - It is easy for me to be humble. **Answers will vary, but it is most often difficult for us to stay humble. We need constant reminders from God.**
   - Herod's humility helped him rule the Jews. **Herod was arrogant and evil. These traits were passed along to his son, Archelaus, who ruled after him. The Roman Emperor, Augustus, punished Archelaus for his cruelty by banishing him from Palestine to Gaul (today's France).**
   - Arrogance will get you further in life than humility. **This is a worldly perspective that seems to work initially but never in the long run.**
5. Unlike people, God always keeps his promise. Evidence can be found throughout Scripture of this reality.
6. God speaks in many ways to us today—through Scripture, in prayer, through sermons, through other Christians, and through the circumstances we find ourselves in.

THE CLOSE
God is a God who speaks to us each and every day. In creation, God tells us of his mighty power to order and rule the universe. Through the people he places in our lives each day, God lets us learn things like patience and kindness. As we read the Bible, God speaks to us about what he wants us to do. In prayer, God nudges us in new directions. God is intimately involved in talking with us every day.

1. Which of the following describes you?

- ☐ Been baptized
- ☐ Became a church member
- ☐ Taken communion
- ☐ Own a Bible
- ☐ Gone to Vacation Bible School
- ☐ Memorized at least 10 Bible verses
- ☐ Participated in a Christmas play

5. Luke 2:21-40

JESUS GROWS UP

God wants us to be mature Christians,
so let's grow up in our faith

2. Finish this sentence:

A "baby Christian" is someone who—

3. What do you think about the following statements—do you A (agree) or D (disagree)?

___ I have to be an adult before I can mature as a Christian.
___ Only those who pray an hour each day are growing Christians.
___ The church is filled with baby Christians.
___ Growing as a Christian means I have to give up having fun.
___ I have no idea what it means to grow in my faith.
___ Growing Christians will only date other Christians who are growing in their faith.
___ Growing Christians walk their talk.
___ If you aren't growing in your faith, God loves you less.
___ Growing in Christ means three steps forward and two steps back.
___ Christian growth takes time.
___ Christians become who they hang around with.

4. The Bible says Simeon was a man who loved the Lord. God allowed him to see Jesus before he died. As a mature believer, what advice do you think Simeon would give you about growing closer to Jesus Christ? Who at your church is like Simeon?

5. In the space below, name all the people you know who are like Anna (people who pray and pray for others).

6. How will you know when you are a mature Christian? What do you think you will enjoy most about being a mature Christian?

READ OUT LOUD
Exodus 13:2 required that every Jewish family present their firstborn male child to God along with an offering. So Joseph and Mary head to the temple to do the right thing. Read the story found in Luke 2:21-40.

ASK
What is the first really big "mature" thing you did?

DISCUSS, BY THE NUMBERS
1. Each of these activities describes a "growth" experience that many people go through as young people. Joseph and Mary dedicated Jesus to God. Ask, "How have your family or Christian friends helped you become more committed to Christ?"
2. Get a group definition of a baby Christian. Say, "We don't need to stay baby Christians; we can grow up in our faith in Jesus Christ."
3. See commentary in bold after each statement.
   - I have to be an adult before I can mature as a Christian. **No, there are many young people who are more mature than adults.**
   - Only those who pray an hour each day are growing Christians. **Encourage young people *not* to get hung up on time slots for growth. Rather, look at opportunities for growth through praying often and other activities.**
   - The church is filled with baby Christians. **Great to debate this one. Talk about what to do about it.**
   - Growing as a Christian means I have to give up having fun. **This is a myth. Christians have more fun because there are not the negative consequences to pay like hangovers, unwanted pregnancies, or school suspensions for fighting.**
   - I have no idea what it means to grow in my faith. **Agreeing with this statement is an honest response.**
   - Growing Christians will only date other Christians who are growing in their faith. **A good one to debate. Do talk about the dangers of "evangelism dating"—that is, dating people who don't have faith in Christ hoping you can convert them.**
   - Growing Christians walk their talk. **Yes!**
   - If you are not growing in your faith, God loves you less. **Not at all. There is nothing you can do to make God love you any more or less.**
   - Growing in Christ means three steps forward and two steps back. **This is often true.**
   - Christian growth takes time. **Yes. While conversion is instantaneous, growth is a process over time.**
   - Christians become who they hang around with. **Yes, so hang around Christians who are growing. This does not mean you shouldn't have friendships with those who don't follow Christ—but be aware of the negative influence they can have on you.**
4. You'll be surprised by the maturity in the answers your group members will give to both of these questions.
5. Ask, "How can you become more like the people you identified?"
6. Identify a set of indicators that measure Christian maturity—things like regular prayer and Bible reading; evidence of the fruit of the Spirit (Galatians 5:22-23); involvement in Christ's body, the church.

THE CLOSE
Just like you wouldn't want to stay a kid your whole life, you don't want to stay a kid Christian forever. Now is a great time to get going and growing in your faith.

1. Like every good Jewish family, Jesus' family participated in Passover every year.

   What spiritual traditions does your family do together?

   - We talk often about Jesus at home.
   - We read the Bible together at least weekly.
   - We pray together every day.
   - Other: _____

   _____

THE TEENAGE JESUS

Everyone grows physically, emotionally, spiritually, and mentally

2. Read the statement about Jesus' teenage years and decide if you A (agree) or D (disagree).

   ___ Jesus knew that he was God when he was born.
   ___ Jesus studied the Bible often as a teenager.
   ___ Jesus had disagreements with his brothers and mother.
   ___ Jesus performed miracles as a teenager.
   ___ Jesus didn't pray much as a teenager.

3. Jesus' parents worried about him when they didn't need to. When have your parents worried about you when they didn't need to? When have your parents worried about you when they did need to?

4. How was growing up the same in Jesus' time as it is today?

   - Jesus' body changed as he grew up just like my body.
   - Jesus wrestled with spiritual issues just like I have.
   - Jesus had all kinds of feelings just as I have had.
   - Jesus faced challenges with his family similar to the ones I have faced.
   - Jesus learned the trade of carpentry from his father just like I have to learn certain skills for a career.
   - Jesus had pressure from his friends to sin.
   - Jesus faced tough choices just like I have.
   - Jesus could have had acne problems, crooked teeth, or vision problems.
   - Jesus was athletic and muscular but not the best-looking guy as a teenager.

5. What do you think Jesus did as a teenager that made God so happy? How happy is God with the direction of your life?

And as Jesus grew up,
he increased in wisdom and in favor with God and people. (Luke 2:52)

READ OUT LOUD

Christ, as God, became human. And as a person, Christ experienced the developmental stages of life—infancy, childhood, adolescence, and adulthood. Jesus, as a teenager, developed physically (voice changed, acne appeared), emotionally (a sometimes roller coaster), spiritually (became aware of his relationship with God and finally that he is God), and mentally (learned more and more). Read the story from Luke 2:41-52.

ASK

What do you think is the hardest part about growing up? The easiest part?

DISCUSS, BY THE NUMBERS

1. Share a story of one of your spiritual traditions. Talk about a tradition that involves Jesus. Let your group members talk about their special spiritual traditions. Ask, "Why do you think it is important to have spiritual traditions?" Possible answers: They remind us of our spiritual heritage; they draw us closer to God.

    For group members who don't have traditions that involve Christianity, talk about ways they can engage their families in traditions that involve Jesus. This is also a good time to talk about ways to get their parents and family to check out Jesus and your congregation.

2. See commentary in bold after each statement.
    - Jesus knew that he was God when he was born. **No. Jesus had a growing awareness of his deity that didn't fully develop until he was an adult.**
    - Jesus studied the Bible often as a teenager. **Jesus knew the Old Testament, the Bible of his time. He knew it so well that his understanding of it surprised the Bible teachers of that time.**
    - Jesus had disagreements with his brothers and mother. **Yes. Jesus had disagreements with his mother and brothers in childhood and adulthood without sinning. You can disagree agreeably without sinning.**
    - Jesus performed miracles as a teenager. **He could have performed small miracles privately for his family if they were experiencing financial hardship. We just don't know. We know his first *public* miracle was turning water into wine at a wedding party.**
    - Jesus didn't pray much as a teenager. **Based on what we see of his adult life, Jesus would have prayed often as a teenager.**

3. Talk about ways your group members can assure their parents that their lives are going well. This is a trust issue. If one of your group members has broken trust with a parent, it will take time (more time than a teenager wishes) for that trust to be earned back.

4. See Isaiah 53 for a description of Jesus. Talk about the challenges your group members face as teenagers. Jesus' youth was similar in many ways to that of your group members. He was free from sin but did face the same trials and tribulations faced by young people today.

5. Read Luke 2:52 out loud. Ask your group members to comment on the questions: "What do you think Jesus did as a teenager that made God so happy?" and, "How happy is God with the direction of your life?"

And as Jesus grew up,
he increased in wisdom and in favor with God and people. (Luke 2:52)

THE CLOSE

Growing up is about, well, growing. As you move from childhood to adulthood you grow physically, emotionally, spiritually, and mentally, just like Jesus did. That's the nice thing about serving a God who became a person—Jesus understands what it's like to become an adult. Body not quite what you want? Jesus understands. Feelings sometimes messed up? Jesus understands. Spiritually confused? Jesus understands. Brain power not what you would like? Jesus understands.

1. **Check the box after each statement that best describes you.**

	Always	Mostly	Sometimes	Never
• My sins are disgustingly evil.	❏	❏	❏	❏
• I'm so, so sorry for my sins. I regret what I have done to offend God.	❏	❏	❏	❏
• I have sinned against Jesus and caused his death.	❏	❏	❏	❏
• I ask God to forgive me of my sins.	❏	❏	❏	❏
• My sins will lead to a life of misery.	❏	❏	❏	❏
• I want to turn my life around and live a holy life.	❏	❏	❏	❏
• I want to be part of God's kingdom rather than Satan's kingdom.	❏	❏	❏	❏

7. Matthew 4:18-22

THE FIRST DISCIPLES GO WITH JESUS

Jesus wants us to follow him into a life of promise and purpose

2. **To me, following Jesus means—**
   - Getting whatever I want when I pray
   - Making more money
   - A life filled with purpose
   - A life of hardship and pain
   - I can have a cool car
   - Unimaginable joy
   - A promise of eternal life

3. **Each of the following Bible passages has a promise attached for following Christ. All five are important. Which of the five appeals to you most right now?**
   - John 14:27
   - Matthew 11:28
   - John 6:40
   - John 10:10
   - Hebrews 2:17

4. **The disciples left their comfort zones for the unknown to follow Jesus. How serious are you about following Christ?**

	Yes	No	Maybe
• I am willing to stay single if necessary to follow Jesus.	❏	❏	❏
• I am willing to change friends if necessary to follow Jesus.	❏	❏	❏
• I am willing to make less money if necessary to follow Jesus.	❏	❏	❏
• I am willing to be made fun of if necessary to follow Jesus.	❏	❏	❏
• I am willing to go wherever if necessary to follow Jesus.	❏	❏	❏

5. **Why do you think Christ asked 12 ordinary people, rather than religious leaders, to be his first followers?**

READ OUT LOUD

Jesus asked 12 people to follow him closely. These 12, called disciples, followed him for three years. Jesus started his ministry near Nazareth, the town in which he was raised, in a region of Israel called Galilee. There he asked the first four of the 12 disciples to follow and learn from him. Read the story from Matthew 4:18-22.

ASK

Who or what do most people follow today?

DISCUSS, BY THE NUMBERS

1. See commentary in bold after each statement.
   - My sins are disgustingly evil. **In God's eyes all sin is disgustingly evil because it misses his mark of holiness.**
   - I'm so, so sorry for my sins. I regret what I have done to offend God. **This is the first part of repentance. The second part is turning your life around to go in a new direction.**
   - I have sinned against Jesus and caused his death. **Yes, we did contribute to Jesus' death on the cross.**
   - I ask God to forgive me of my sins. **A necessary step in following Jesus.**
   - My sins will lead to a life of misery. **Yes, the consequence of continuing to lead a life of sin apart from Christ is misery.**
   - I want to turn my life around and live a holy life. **This is the second part of repentance.**
   - I want to be part of God's kingdom rather than Satan's kingdom. **Jesus preached repentance because the kingdom of heaven (or kingdom of God) was upon us. When he taught the disciples to pray, he said to God, "Your kingdom come, your will be done on earth..." We're either a part of God's kingdom here on Earth or Satan's. The choice is ours.**

2. Listen to the completed sentences by asking your group members which of the boxes they checked. Following Christ is not about getting what we want but about receiving a life of promise and purpose—something only Christ can give.

3. See which of the Bible promises appealed to your group members. Encourage your group members with these promises.

4. To lead a life of promise and purpose requires that we move out of our comfort zones. The Bible is filled with stories of people of faith moving out of their comfort zones into a more exciting life. See how serious your group members are about following Jesus. Tell a story from your life that shows how following Christ gives you a life of promise and purpose.

5. This is a great question to debate. Christ's choice of the 12 gives us hope of being followers of Jesus today. We don't have to be religious to follow Jesus. We need only to want a relationship with God to be a Christ-follower.

THE CLOSE

An exciting life of promise and purpose is what we receive when we choose to follow Jesus. It's not always an easy life. It's not always a fun-every-minute life. It's not always a problem-free life. But it's a life you will never regret!

JESUS WORKS A NEEDED WEDDING MIRACLE

Bringing our needs to Jesus, who is Lord of our lives

1. **Question Bombardment.** Many people put their faith in Christ after he showed signs of his authority as God through miracles. What do you think influenced people to believe in him before he performed miracles? What influenced you to trust in Jesus Christ? If you haven't put your faith in Christ, in what have you put your faith? What would it take for you to trust in Christ?

2. The story illustrates that Jesus had a good time with people, including his disciples, and he wants to have a good time with us.

   • Jesus wants us to have a good time with him because . . .

   • I have had a good time with Jesus by . . .

   • I invite Jesus to come with me when I have a good time with my friends because . . .

3. Mary went from a mother-son relationship with Jesus to a sinner-Lord relationship. How tough do you think this transition was for Mary? How tough has it been for you to live your life with Jesus, rather than you, in charge?

4. Running out of refreshments at the wedding celebration would have been embarrassing to the family. Mary, a friend of the family, wanted to help but had no solution on her own other than to apologize to the guests. She decides to go to Jesus and . . . (circle one answer)

   a. ask him to make an excuse to the guests for the lack of wine.
   b. tell him of the problem as well as what she thinks would be a good solution.
   c. tell him only of the problem.
   d. give him money to go buy more wine.

5. Do you think these statements are T (true) or F (false)?

   ___ God wants me to suggest to him the solutions to my problems so he can implement my solutions.
   ___ If you gave only your concerns to God without your suggested solutions, your prayer time would be cut in half.
   ___ God always answers my prayers with the right answer for me.
   ___ It's not always easy to accept God's answers to my prayers.
   ___ Our solutions to our problems are often the same as God's solutions.

6. How much wine do you think Jesus drank? Would he have gotten drunk? Why or why not?

READ OUT LOUD

This story describes the beginning of Jesus' public ministry. It is important to note that Jesus began his ministry in an indistinct corner of Palestine away from Jerusalem, the hub of the country and its political and religious life. Jesus goes first to "Joe Average" before going to the popular people. First-century wedding celebrations in Israel lasted up to a week. These monster parties with large guest lists were neighborhood blowout celebrations. It is at this party that Jesus performed his first public miracle. Bible scholars consider this miracle the official beginning of Jesus' public ministry. Read the Jesus party story out loud from John 2:1-11.

ASK

Where do you go to shop when you need new clothes?

DISCUSS, BY THE NUMBERS

1. Christ's miracles had a sacred purpose—to point to him as the One who was Messiah God, the Savior of the world. The miracles of Jesus were signs of his authority as God. That's why, so often, the religious leaders stirred up the people to stone him. Jesus said he was God; that was blasphemous to the Jews.
2. Ask, "What picture forms in your head when you think of Jesus as the God-person who liked to party?" Give several group members the chance to share their completed sentences.
3. Jesus' mom, Mary, asked him to help her friends in the wedding party who had unexpectedly run out of wine. The guests would be leaving sooner than desired because of the lack of refreshments. Jesus chose this time, the beginning of his public ministry, to change his relationship with his mom. His reply to his mother, saying that she must not tell him what to do, indicated the change. No longer would they be mother and son. Now they would be sinner and Lord and Savior. Talk with your group about decisions that must be made daily to make Jesus Lord of their lives.
4. "C" is the answer. Mary brought the need, and only the need, to Jesus. She didn't tell Jesus how to fix the situation.

5. See commentary in bold after each statement.
- God wants me to suggest to him the solutions to my problems so he can implement my solutions. **God wants us to boldly come to him with our needs. Then, God wants us to trust in him for the solutions. It's all about making Jesus Lord of our lives.**
- If you gave only your concerns to God without your suggested solutions, your prayer time would be cut in half. **Excluding our proposed solutions to God makes our prayer life much easier (and a little shorter).**
- God always answers my prayers with the right answer for me. **True, but it is not always the answer we want. Sometimes the answer is "wait and wait and wait," which can be the hardest of all the answers.**
- It's not always easy to accept God's answers to my prayers. **Accepting God's solution to our prayer requests gets easier the longer we make Jesus Lord of our lives. We begin to see that his solutions work out better than our solutions!**
- Our solutions to our problems are often the same as God's solutions. **Sometimes yes, sometimes no! We would like to think that our solutions would be best. Fortunately, we serve a big, big God who can see the big picture of our lives.**

THE CLOSE

How often in our prayer lives do we come to God with our concerns as well as propose a solution to God? What would it take for us to go to Christ with only our needs and the needs of others, trusting that his solution is the right one? We need not be prescriptive with Christ, only descriptive of our problems. To trust in Christ means to let go of our control and give that control to Christ just like his mom, Mary, did. Giving God our concerns without attaching our solution to the request takes practice. Begin now!

NOTE: JESUS' MIRACLE GIVES YOU THE OPPORTUNITY TO DIALOGUE WITH YOUR GROUP MEMBERS ABOUT DRINKING ALCOHOL.

1. **Jesus partied with slimy lowlifes like Levi. Who do you think people today view as the slimy lowlifes of our society? (Pick the top three.)**

A BIG DINNER WITH SINNERS

God's grace is available to everyone

- ☐ Prostitutes
- ☐ Drug dealers
- ☐ Politicians
- ☐ Homosexuals
- ☐ Convicted felons
- ☐ Bankers
- ☐ Car dealers
- ☐ Homeless people
- ☐ Professional athletes
- ☐ Gang bangers
- ☐ Lawyers
- ☐ Celebrities
- ☐ Unmarried couples who live together

2. **Why do you think Levi wanted Jesus to meet all of his slimy, lowlife friends?**

- He needed Jesus to turn water into wine for the party.
- He thought it would be good for Jesus and the disciples to hang out with the cool people.
- He wanted to see how much Jesus could drink.
- He wanted his friends to hear the good news that Jesus was preaching.
- He wanted to see if he could get Jesus to sin.
- He thought Jesus and the disciples should quit being so "goody two-shoes."
- He wanted to hook Jesus up.

3. **Why do you think Levi would give up a high-paying job with all the benefits to follow Jesus?**

- Because making money is a sin
- Because Jesus had become the most important thing in his life
- Because pleasure doesn't satisfy
- Because Jesus promised to teach him how to surf
- Because he realized that Jesus was the way, the truth, and the life
- Because Jesus asked the right questions along with giving the right answers
- Because he wanted more out of life than drinking, pleasure, and riches

4. **What do you think the disciples of Jesus who attended Levi's party were thinking?**

- "Cool party! Jesus rocks!!"
- "Wow, Jesus will forgive anyone who turns to him."
- "I've got a lot to learn about agape love."
- "Women shouldn't dress like that!"
- "God's grace is really big!"
- "Where's the hand sanitizer?"
- "Jesus can't possibly forgive the sins of the slimeballs at this party."

5. **Jesus rubbed shoulders with the culture of his day. How can you get Jesus into the world of your school, your job, or your sports team without the ways of the world getting into you?**

READ OUT LOUD

The people hated Levi because, as a tax collector, he would cheat people out of more money than they owed the government for their taxes. The Roman soldiers would back the tax collectors because they received a cut of the money. He was invited by Jesus to follow him. Levi said yes and threw a big party so that all his friends could hear what Jesus had to say. Read the story found in Luke 5:27-32. Oh yeah, Levi was also named Matthew, who became one of Christ's 12 and wrote the Gospel of Matthew.

ASK

With whom would you never want to have dinner?

DISCUSS, BY THE NUMBERS

1. Talk about why Jesus would want to invite such a despicable sinner like Levi to follow him.
2. Why do you think Levi wanted Jesus to meet all of his slimy, low-life friends? The answer: He wanted his friends to hear the good news that Jesus was preaching.
3. See commentary in bold after each statement.
   - Because making money is a sin. **Making money is not a sin, but the love of money is!**
   - Because Jesus had become the most important thing in his life. **Jesus did become the most important thing in his life.**
   - Because pleasure doesn't satisfy. **And Matthew had this one figured out. He was empty and tired of the shallow things in life.**
   - Because Jesus promised to teach him how to surf. **No evidence for this one, but it could have been cool to surf with Jesus.**
   - Because he realized that Jesus was the way, the truth, and the life. **Yes—ask, "Why are some people able to figure this out while others want to keep living for themselves?"**

   - Because Jesus asked the right questions, along with giving the right answers. **The crowds were amazed by both Jesus' questions and answers.**
   - Because he wanted more out of life than drinking, pleasure, and riches. **Again, the emptiness of selfish living had caught up with Levi, and he wanted something more.**
4. See commentary in bold after each statement.
   - "Cool party! Jesus rocks!!" **Maybe.**
   - "Wow, Jesus will forgive anyone who turns to him." **Probably.**
   - "I've got a lot to learn about agape love." **Most likely.**
   - "Women shouldn't dress like that!" **Could have.**
   - "God's grace is really big!" **Most definitely.**
   - "Where's the hand sanitizer?" **At times, maybe.**
   - "Jesus can't possibly forgive the sins of the slimeballs at this party." **Hopefully not!**
5. We have to figure out how to live in the world without the world living in us.

THE CLOSE

Levi became the disciple named Matthew. He kept following Jesus and never looked back. He left everything about his old life and entered a new adventure with Jesus. The grace and mercy of God saved Levi and turned him into "Matthew." Are you letting God's grace change you?

THE FAITH OF A ROMAN ARMY OFFICER

Our faith in Christ can grow stronger

1. The friends of the Roman army officer went to Jesus for him.

   How often do you pray for your friends?
   ❏ All the time ❏ Not often enough ❏ Rarely or never

   Your family and other relatives?
   ❏ All the time ❏ Not often enough ❏ Rarely or never

2. Why do you think the Roman army officer had a synagogue built for the Jews? Do you think he may have worshiped there?

3. Like the Roman army officer, I am unworthy of Christ's attention and concern.

   Agree   Disagree

4. Jesus recognized the strong faith displayed by the Roman army officer. What kind of faith does Jesus see in you?

   ❏ No faith   ❏ A weak faith   ❏ A growing faith that needs to be energized   ❏ A strong and growing faith

5. How well do you practice the ways of faith?

1	2	3	4	5	6	7	8	9	10

Pray all the time   Don't pray at all

1	2	3	4	5	6	7	8	9	10

Read the Bible often   Never read the Bible

1	2	3	4	5	6	7	8	9	10

Talk often with friends   Never talk with friends
about my faith   about my faith

1	2	3	4	5	6	7	8	9	10

Worship regularly   Never worship
with my congregation   with my congregation

1	2	3	4	5	6	7	8	9	10

Often serve   Never serve
those in need   those in need

READ OUT LOUD

Christ recognizes a Roman army officer—someone not known for trusting in the God of the Jews—for his strong faith. The army officer cared about the Jews because he had built them a synagogue, a place for them to worship God together. Jesus was surprised by the faith that he showed and did something special for him. Read the story from Luke 7:1-10.

ASK

What sport would you say requires the most strength?

DISCUSS, BY THE NUMBERS

1. The army officer really cared about his servant. And his friends knew that and went to Jesus on behalf of the army officer. Ask, "Why do you think it is important to have friends praying for you? Why is it important for you to regularly pray for your friends?"
2. Let your group speculate about the faith habits of the army officer. Perhaps he had at least toyed with becoming a Jew. Maybe he did worship at the synagogue with the Jews. Some of his servants were most likely Jews, and they probably talked with him about the God of the Bible or even Jesus.
3. The army officer sensed his brokenness; he felt guilty because of his sin. We must humbly recognize our sinfulness as we approach Christ. At the same time we must recognize that Jesus thought we were worth dying for!
4. Any of the four responses can get a faith conversation going. Talk about how our faith needs to be energized on a regular basis. This is why we come together as a church. We encourage each other in the faith. We tell stories of how God is working in our lives. We pray for each other. We worship God together. All this and more energizes our faith as we grow in our relationship with Christ.
5. Prayer, Bible reading, faith conversations, corporate worship, and service are five of the many spiritual disciplines we practice as Christians to grow stronger in our faith in Christ. Use these line scales to see how your group members are doing at practicing the ways of the Christian faith.

THE CLOSE

The Bible tells us that Jesus was amazed at the strong faith of the army officer, and at the lack of faith on the part of the people in his hometown of Nazareth. This is a contrast worth noting because it teaches us that we have a choice. We can amaze Christ by our growing faith or by our lack of faith. What will it be for you?

1. If I had seen Jesus raise the boy to life, I would have—

JESUS RAISES A WIDOW'S SON TO LIFE

Jesus is a compassionate God who loves you

2. How would you answer these—Y (yes) or N (no)?

____ Is raising a boy from the dead proof that Jesus is God?

____ Will anyone who looks seriously at the evidence conclude that Jesus is God?

____ Do atheists have just as good an argument that there is no God as Christians do for the existence of Jesus?

____ Are there people who will, no matter what you say or do, never put their faith in Jesus?

____ Do you think Jesus is who he says he is?

3. Do you A (agree) or D (disagree) with each of the statements below?

____ Jesus cares more about you than you care about yourself.

____ Jesus can handle most of your worries.

____ Jesus wants you to pray more about your concerns.

____ Jesus doesn't want to be bothered with your little problems.

____ Jesus loves only those who have put their faith in him.

4. Is the good news about Jesus spreading in your—

• extended family?	☐ Yes	☐ No	☐ Maybe
• school?	☐ Yes	☐ No	☐ Maybe
• community?	☐ Yes	☐ No	☐ Maybe

5. The people who witnessed or heard about the miraculous resurrection of the boy by Jesus were frightened. Why do you think a healthy fear of God could be good for you?

READ OUT LOUD

The custom, at the time of Jesus, was to carry a corpse in an open-boxed coffin to the gravesite. People would follow along, mourning for the dead. This custom is still observed today. Maybe you've seen a Middle Eastern funeral on the news. Jesus was entering Nain, a small town in the province of Galilee, with a large crowd following him, when he ran into a funeral procession. Read what happens in Luke 7:11-17.

ASK

What do you have to do to get one of your parents to use your full name?

DISCUSS, BY THE NUMBERS

1. Have fun with this item so that you prime the pump for faith conversations about Jesus' power and compassion.
2. See commentary in bold after each question.
   - Is raising a boy from the dead proof that Jesus is God? **It was for the people at the time of Jesus. Ask, "Is it proof enough for you?"**
   - Will anyone who looks seriously at the evidence conclude that Jesus is God? **Some do and some don't. Ask why.**
   - Do atheists have just as good an argument that there is no God as Christians do for the existence of Jesus? **You can't prove there is no God. There is, however, factual evidence for the existence of Jesus and his resurrection.**
   - Are there people who will, no matter what you say or do, never put their faith in Jesus? **Yes.**
   - Do you think Jesus is who he says he is? **This is the question that decides one's eternity.**
3. Do you **A (agree)** or **D (disagree)** with each of the statements below?
   - Jesus cares more about you than you care about yourself. **Yes, Jesus does. And because of this compassion, you can care about others.**
   - Jesus can handle most of your worries. **Jesus can handle all your worries (see 1 Peter 5:7).**
   - Jesus wants you to pray more about your concerns. **Yes, because prayer is nothing more than a conversation with God.**
   - Jesus doesn't want to be bothered with your little problems. **To Jesus there is no such thing as a little problem. There are problems, however, that you can easily do something about—Jesus does want you to use your brain to solve problems.**
   - Jesus loves only those who have put their faith in him. **Jesus loves all of humanity and is heartbroken by those who don't put their faith in him (see 2 Peter 3:9).**
4. News about Jesus seemed to always spread quickly. Examine how news is spreading about Jesus because of the way your group members are living.
5. Talk about a healthy fear of (or respect for) God. While God is approachable because of the forgiveness Jesus offers and we can count Jesus as a friend, God is still God and deserves our respect.

THE CLOSE

Jesus shows his divinity and power by raising a widow's son to life in front of a crowd of his followers. Jesus shows his followers, by this act of caring, that they also need to care about others who are hurting. Jesus shows us today that in a world filled with hurt, we, too, need to be compassionate.

1. Check the best definition of *self-righteous*.

- ☐ To believe you're better than others
- ☐ To arrogantly see yourself as really cool
- ☐ To be a holier-than-thou goody-goody hypocrite
- ☐ To be intolerant of what others think or believe
- ☐ To be pharisaical, or like a Pharisee

JESUS ANOINTED BY A SINFUL WOMAN

How broken do you think you really are?

2. Check the best definition of *spiritual brokenness*.

- ☐ To realize that you have sinned against a holy God
- ☐ To see yourself as God sees you
- ☐ To understand that you can never be good enough to be acceptable to God
- ☐ To have a humble and repentant spirit
- ☐ To admit that your life is a mess when lived under your control

3. On the scale below, where would you rank yourself in your brokenness?

■☐☐■

I am totally broken — I am really powerful & in control

4. Question Bombardment: What has been your response to God's forgiveness of your sins? Have you asked for forgiveness? Once you ask for forgiveness, can you do anything you want? How often do you need to ask for forgiveness? Once you've asked for forgiveness of a sin, do you need to keep asking? Do you need to ask for forgiveness for sins you don't know you committed? Do you need to forgive others when they sin against you? How often do you need to forgive others?

"Your faith has saved you; go in peace."
—Jesus to the woman, in Luke 7:50

5. Our society doesn't talk much about sin today. Why do you think this is so? Check your top-two reasons.

- ☐ People don't believe their sins are that bad.
- ☐ Because sin is fun.
- ☐ Hey, what happens in Vegas, stays in Vegas.
- ☐ Our society doesn't want to take responsibility for bad behaviors.
- ☐ We like to glorify sin rather than condemn it.
- ☐ If it feels good, how can it be a sin?
- ☐ We don't think there is a hell.
- ☐ If the good we do outweighs our sins, then God will accept us.
- ☐ When sin is minimized there is no need for a solution to sin.

The other guests began to say among themselves,
"Who is this who even forgives sins?" (Luke 7:49)

READ OUT LOUD

A Pharisee named Simon invited Jesus to his home for dinner. Jesus probably had healed Simon of leprosy, and this was the celebratory thank-you meal.* This is a story of two types of gratitude—one of a self-righteous Pharisee and the other of a broken sinner saved by grace. Read the story from Luke 7:36-50.

ASK

Are you more or less important than your friends think you are?

DISCUSS, BY THE NUMBERS

1. Each of the statements describes self-righteousness. Talk about each and come up with a group definition.

2. Check the best definition of *spiritual brokenness*. As in item #1, each of the statements describes spiritual brokenness. Talk about each and again come up with a group definition.

3. The sinful woman recognized her brokenness, the greatness of her sins. She saw herself as a broken sinner who desperately needed Jesus, her Savior. It is critical to realize you are broken before you can accept God's free gift of salvation. Simon seemed to think he didn't need grace—that his good works as a Pharisee could save him without Jesus. We must come to Jesus broken. Those who don't come to Jesus think they are in control of their own lives, an illusion that can be believed all of one's life. Ask, "Why do you think some people refuse to see their brokenness—to want to stay in control of their lives?"

4. All of the questions in this Question Bombardment speak to forgiveness, the act that follows our recognition of brokenness. Once we recognize that we are sinners, we can ask for and receive Christ's forgiveness. Christ forgave the woman's sins because she knew she was broken. The sinful woman loved the Lord because her sins were forgiven. Her love was her response to Christ's forgiveness. Her faith in Christ's ability to forgive her (not any work or action on her part, but the work done by Christ) saved her.

5. See commentary in bold after each statement.
   - People don't believe their sins are *that* bad. **In this 21st century, many people only look at sin as sin if they perceive it to be a really-big-awful-and-evil-something. They don't see sin as God sees sin—anything that misses God's mark of holiness.**
   - Because sin is fun. **Sin can be fun for a short period of time. It's those pesky consequences that quickly stop the fun.**
   - Hey, what happens in Vegas, stays in Vegas. **This attitude actually celebrates sin.**
   - Our society doesn't want to take responsibility for bad behaviors. **Our society likes to rationalize, blame others, or minimize responsibility for bad behaviors.**
   - We like to glorify sin rather than condemn it. **Yes, as in, you are cool for doing something bad.**
   - If it feels good, how can it be a sin? **The permissiveness of our culture says, "If it feels good, do it."**
   - We don't think there is a hell. **If there is no hell, there is no ultimate consequence for sin.**
   - If the good we do outweighs our sins, then God will accept us. **This salvation through good works minimizes sin and negates the need for the cross.**
   - When sin is minimized there is no need for a solution to sin. **And then you don't have to submit to Jesus.**

THE CLOSE

When people recognize their sin as a problem, then they want something to be done about it. That's when people are ready to turn to Christ. Recognizing brokenness is the necessary prerequisite for salvation. We can learn something from Alcoholics Anonymous about brokenness. The first step toward recovery from an addiction to alcohol, other drugs, or any addictive behavior is admitting powerlessness. Here is the first step applied to sin: "We admitted we were powerless over our sin, that our sin had made our lives unmanageable." Once we can admit that our sin has gotten the best of us, then are ready to need a Savior.

*See Mark 14:3.

THE STORY OF A FARMER

Talking the good news with all kinds of people

1. I can share the good news with others—
O (often), S (sometimes), or N (never)

___ by acting like I'm a Christian.

___ by telling others about Jesus' love and forgiveness.

___ by the way I speak.

___ by what I wear.

___ by how hard I study.

___ by the kind of music I listen to.

___ by how I use my time.

___ by who I hang out with.

___ by how I treat my family and friends.

___ by the kinds of movies I watch.

After this, Jesus traveled about from one town and village to another, proclaiming the good news of the kingdom of God. The Twelve were with him… (Luke 8:1)

2. Finish this statement: The devil can—

This is the meaning of the parable: The seed is the word of God. Those along the path are the ones who hear, and then the devil comes and takes away the word from their hearts, so that they may not believe and be saved.—Jesus, in Luke 8:11-12

3. Check out these statements and decide if each is T (true) or F (false).

___You can tell those who become Christians because their lives change.

___When people lose interest in Christ, it's our job to reintroduce them to the gospel.

___A superficial belief in Christ is not faith in Christ.

___I know someone who heard the gospel with excitement but then lost interest in Jesus.

___When times get tough, most people lose interest in Christ.

Those on the rock are the ones who receive the word with joy when they hear it, but they have no root. They believe for a while, but in the time of testing they fall away.—Jesus, in Luke 8:13

4. What do you think "chokes" the good news of Christ out of people's lives? (Check your top three.)

☐ Pleasure

☐ Entertainment

☐ Thrill-seeking

☐ Alcohol & other drugs like marijuana

☐ Worrying too much

☐ Romance

☐ Money

☐ Sports

☐ Internet

☐ Wanting more

The seed that fell among thorns stands for those who hear, but as they go on their way they are choked by life's worries, riches and pleasures, and they do not mature.—Jesus, in Luke 8:14

5. How are you a "good soil" kind of person? How do you know?

But the seed on good soil stands for those with a noble and good heart, who hear the word, retain it, and by persevering produce a crop.—Jesus, in Luke 8:15

READ OUT LOUD

Once upon a time there was a farmer. Jesus tells a famous story that you've probably heard before. Jesus wants his disciples to understand that they need to tell others the good news but that they are not responsible for how people respond to that good news. Read the story found in Luke 8:1-15.

ASK

What plant do you think has the weirdest-looking seed?

DISCUSS, BY THE NUMBERS

1. Whether they mean to or not, Christians share the good news of Jesus all the time. Even when they're not speaking to others about spiritual things, they're "witnessing" by how they treat others, what they say, or how well they do in school. Unfortunately much of the time they're clueless that people who aren't believers are watching how they act, how they talk, etc. Read Luke 8:1 out loud. Examine each of the statements to see what message your group members are giving about Jesus.

After this, Jesus traveled about from one town and village to another, proclaiming the good news of the kingdom of God. The Twelve were with him. (Luke 8:1)

2. Quote Jesus out loud from Luke 8:11-12. Listen to the completed sentences. Christ desires that everyone find salvation. The devil works for the opposite goal to be achieved.

This is the meaning of the parable: The seed is the word of God. Those along the path are the ones who hear, and then the devil comes and takes away the word from their hearts, so that they may not believe and be saved.—Jesus, in Luke 8:11-12

3. Quote Jesus out loud from Luke 8:13. See commentary in bold after each statement.

Those on the rock are the ones who receive the word with joy when they hear it, but they have no root. They believe for a while, but in the time of testing they fall away. —Jesus, in Luke 8:13

- You can tell those who've become Christians because their lives change. **Yes, the seed fell on good rather than rocky soil.**
- When people lose interest in Christ, it's our job to reintroduce them to the gospel. **The initial emotional excitement may disappear, but they still may want to know more, and yes, it is our job to talk more about Jesus with them.**
- A superficial belief in Christ is not faith in Christ. **There are many people who believe in the existence of Jesus nearly 2,000 years ago but are not Christ-followers.**
- I know someone who heard the gospel with excitement but then lost interest in Jesus. **Rocky soil will do it every time.**
- When times get tough, most people lose interest in Christ. **Some do. That's when the seed fell on rocky soil.**

4. Quote Jesus out loud from Luke 8:14. Decide as a group what is most likely to "choke" the good news of Christ out of the lives of their friends.

The seed that fell among thorns stands for those who hear, but as they go on their way they are choked by life's worries, riches and pleasures, and they do not mature. —Jesus, in Luke 8:14

5. Quote Jesus out loud from Luke 8:15. Talk about people the group members know who are "good soil" kind of people. What made the gospel stick with them?

But the seed on good soil stands for those with a noble and good heart, who hear the word, retain it, and by persevering produce a crop. —Jesus, in Luke 8:15

THE CLOSE

Like Jesus or his disciples (whom he was teaching through this story), we can do our best to share the good news through our words and our actions. Those we tell who are watching us and listening to us must choose—Jesus or the ways of the world. Let's do the best job we can by talking and walking Jesus and leave the results up to the Holy Spirit.

1. My friends think—

- ☐ They are better than others.
- ☐ They are not as good as others.
- ☐ They are about the same as others.

To some who were confident of their own righteousness and looked down on everyone else, Jesus told this parable...
(Luke 18:9)

2. What type of people can be found in your church?

- ☐ People who go out of their way to help others.
- ☐ People who do things without expecting something in return.
- ☐ People who are arrogant.
- ☐ People who are ignored.
- ☐ People who think their good deeds will get them to heaven.
- ☐ People who enjoy judging and being critical of others.
- ☐ People who want to do the right thing.
- ☐ People who often lie.
- ☐ People who are willing to volunteer.
- ☐ People who love to gossip.
- ☐ People who think only of themselves.
- ☐ People who humbly obey Jesus.

Two men went up to the temple to pray, one a Pharisee and the other a tax collector…—Jesus, in Luke 18:10

3. Finish this statement. The Pharisee—

- ☐ had lived a good life overall.
- ☐ had lived a good life to those who saw him.
- ☐ had lived a sinful, selfish life.

The Pharisee stood by himself and prayed: "God, thank you that I am not like other people—robbers, evildoers, adulterers—or even like this tax collector. I fast twice a week and give a tenth of all I get."—Jesus, in Luke 18:11-12

4. The tax collector felt guilty enough about his sins that he changed his behavior when he left the temple.

_____ I think he did   _____ I don't think he changed

But the tax collector stood at a distance. He would not even look up to heaven, but beat his breast and said, "God, have mercy on me, a sinner." —Jesus, in Luke 18:13

5. Why would God forgive the tax collector for his sins but not the Pharisee?

"I tell you that this man [the tax collector], rather than the other [the Pharisee], went home justified before God. For all those who exalt themselves will be humbled, and those who humble themselves will be exalted." —Jesus, in Luke 18:14

READ OUT LOUD

The Pharisee prayed, away from the sinful tax collector, boasting to God really about the "don'ts" that he hadn't done and the rules he had religiously kept. He certainly was full of himself. And then there was the tax collector, approaching God in fear because of the sins he had committed. Read the story from Luke 18:9-14.

ASK

What do you usually do when you want to be noticed?

DISCUSS, BY THE NUMBERS

1. No matter what your group members' responses, you can talk about the Pharisee thinking he was better than others while the tax collector had a more realistic and humble view of who he was. And remember that Jesus was not talking here about dress, education, or skills but how people see themselves morally. The Pharisee thought he was morally superior while the tax collector saw himself morally guilty of sin that needed forgiveness by God.

2. Both the Pharisee and the tax-collector types of people can be found in your church. Talk about how we move people from seeing themselves as morally superior to others to a biblical view of brokenness and repentance.

3. There are times when we are all like the Pharisee in Jesus' story. We look good outwardly but inwardly are sinful and selfish.

4. We don't know what the tax collector did when he left. Jesus never completes the story. Let your group members make some guesses about what people usually do after they repent.

5. Listen to your group members' answers. Ask, "Would Jesus say you were more like the Pharisee or the tax collector?"

THE CLOSE

How easy it is to act like the Pharisee—we get arrogant and self-righteous. We act as though God is lucky to have us on his team. Like the Pharisee, we don't harm others and we attend church regularly. But is that what living like Jesus is all about—not doing the don'ts and sitting in church? Christ desires a humble and broken heart willing to do whatever Christ wants. Are we there yet?

1. How often would you say our culture pushes us to forgive someone who has wronged us?

■□□□□□□□□□□□□□□□□□□□□□□■

Never forgive   Forgive over
                                 and over

2. Do you **A (agree)** or **D (disagree)** with these statements?

___ Unlimited forgiveness is impossible to pull off.

___ To forgive means to treat the one who asked for forgiveness as though the wrong never happened.

___ People can forgive but not forget.

___ It's easier to forgive as you get older.

___ There are some offenses done to us that are unforgivable.

___ It's easier to forgive those you love than it is your enemies.

___ Forgiveness is easier for Christians than for those who don't know Christ.

3. "The kingdom of heaven is like" refers to God's interactions with his people, the church. How well does your church do with forgiveness?

4. Am I ready to give an account to God for how I have lived my life so far?

☐YES ☐NO ☐MAYBE SO

5. Do you think these statements are **T (true)** or **F (false)**?

___ The king's compassion illustrates how great God's love is for me.

___ Like the servant, I owe God a debt that I can never pay.

___ I live like I am grateful for God's mercy.

___ My sins are like everyone else's sins.

___ I show people who have hurt me the same compassion God shows me.

6. What scares you most about Jesus' response to Peter?

15. Matthew 18:21-35

THE UNFORGIVING GUY

Jesus wants us to forgive and forgive and forgive

READ OUT LOUD

In the Jewish culture, at the time of Jesus, people were taught to forgive three times. After the fourth offense they were no longer required to forgive. The disciple Peter goes overboard and says seven times, which would have been considered incredibly forgiving. Jesus' response would have been shocking to the disciples and is still shocking today. Jesus uses a story to illustrate what he means. Let's read the story from Matthew 18:21-35.

ASK

Who is the most forgiving person you know?

DISCUSS, BY THE NUMBERS

1. Peter, by asking if seven times was enough, was trying to get Jesus to establish the upper limit on forgiveness. Use this line scale to gather your group's opinion regarding our culture's perspective on forgiveness.

2. See commentary in bold next to each statement. Forgiveness, in this story, was to be extended to anyone who asked for it, no matter how many times they asked for it. That is the upside-down kingdom of God. So what about people who never ask for forgiveness? Are we to extend forgiveness to them as well? If you have time, get a faith conversation going about this controversial topic. (Hint: Even if someone never asks for forgiveness, we are to treat them with kindness, never seeking revenge.)

   - Unlimited forgiveness is impossible to pull off. **Apart from the Holy Spirit working in us, it is impossible to pull off. Only through God's help can we forgive again and again and again.**
   - To forgive means to treat the one who asked for forgiveness as though the wrong never happened. **This is a biblical perspective that does not come naturally.**
   - People can forgive but not forget. **Without Christ people can't forget the wrong done to them. It takes supernatural help to do so. Sometimes people do forget things that are too tragic to remember, but they never forgive.**
   - It's easier to forgive as you get older. **A great faith conversation starter statement. See what your group members think!**
   - There are some offenses that are unforgivable. **From a worldly perspective the murder of a friend, rape, and other atrocities seem unforgivable. With Christ any offense against a Christian is forgivable. However, there may be a grieving period from a loss (of life, of innocence) before the act of forgiveness is complete.**
   - It is easier to forgive those you love than your enemies. **This is probably true, but Christ commands us to love our enemies.**

   - Forgiveness is easier for Christians than for those who don't know Christ. **Through the power of Christ this can be true, but only if we surrender to Christ's influence.**

3. See if you can get a group consensus. Talk about the imperfections that exist within God's church. Our goal is to build up the body of Christ until we're all like Jesus (Ephesians 4).

4. The servant was called by the king to account for what he owed. Talk with your group about their readiness to account to God for how they have lived their lives so far. Don't make this a guilt/shame session. Rather, ask your group members to reflect on how they are living their lives and what needs to change for them to live more completely for Christ.

5. See commentary in bold beside each statement.
   - The king's compassion illustrates how great God's love is for me. **The large sum of money owed by the servant demonstrates the greatness of our sins and the extent of God's love in totally forgiving that debt.**
   - Like the servant, I owe God a debt I can never pay. **True. And no amount of good works will pay off that debt. It is only through God's grace that your debt is forgiven.**
   - I live like I am grateful for God's mercy. **Often we take God's grace for granted.**
   - My sins are like everyone else's sins. **Sin is sin. That's why we must forgive others of their sins—because those sins are just like our sins.**
   - I show people who have hurt me the same compassion God shows me. **Since God has forgiven us again and again and again, we need to extend that same mercy to those who have hurt us.**

6. Get responses from your group, then probe for the "why." Often the scariest concept is applying the 70 X 7 rule to life. It's not always easy to forgive again and again and again. It becomes easier when we realize that God's forgiveness shows no limits.

(Note: Matthew 18:34-35 may seem harsh. This is not a picture of what God will do to Christians if they don't forgive. It does make the parable complete, however, and illustrates the importance of forgiveness.)

THE CLOSE

End with this question—***Are you more like the king or the servant in the story?*** Much of the time we are like the servant. We desperately want God to forgive us of our enormous debt of sin, yet we stubbornly refuse to forgive the smallest infractions committed by the ones we love. So who should we aspire to become? Why, Jesus, of course—the giver of grace that's as big as 70 X 7!

1. The lawyer wanted to show Jesus that he knew what he was talking about. He was looking to justify his behavior and prove to Jesus that he had kept the law and deserved a place in heaven. How often do your friends try to justify their inappropriate behavior? How about you?

THE STORY OF THE GOOD SAMARITAN

Who is your neighbor?

2. Through his questions Jesus was leading the lawyer to an understanding of his own sinfulness—a realization that he wasn't able to keep the law and needed a Savior. On the line scale below, place an X where you see yourself.

How aware are you of your brokenness?

| 1 | 2 | 3 | 4 | 5 |

Clueless   Totally aware

3. It would be expected that either the priest or the Levite would have helped the beaten man, a fellow Jew. Why do you think Jesus had them avoid their fellow Jew in need of help? (Choose the one answer you think is most correct.)

- ☐ This might have been a common occurrence.
- ☐ To show that, because they didn't know the person, they didn't feel obligated to see him as their neighbor.
- ☐ One would have to take a risk to help the victim of the robbery.
- ☐ It would cost them money to help the beaten man.
- ☐ Jesus wanted to show that most people have a narrow opinion of who their neighbor is.

4. Do you **A (agree)** or **D (disagree)** with each of these statements?

___ No one today acts like the Samaritan.
___ You'll get sued if you do what the Samaritan did.
___ The victim was just asking to be robbed by traveling alone; he didn't deserve help.
___ There's no reward in being a good Samaritan.
___ I am more like the Samaritan than the priest or Levite.

5. Donnette was so angry. Sara, the girl who sits next to her in Algebra, cheated off her and got caught. Not only did she get her paper taken away, but so did Donnette! Donnette sees Sara crying in the hall. She knows that Sara will probably flunk the class now. What should Donnette say to Sara?

6. Jesus asked the lawyer to identify the neighbor in the story. Who is your neighbor?

READ OUT LOUD

A priest, a Levite, and a Samaritan walk into... No, it's not a joke. It's a story Jesus used to make a point. Jesus was teaching us about our neighbor—specifically about who our neighbor is. A priest at the time was a person from the tribe of Levi whose job was to offer sacrifices to God for the sins of the people. A Levite, again from the tribe of Levi, was the person who assisted the priest in his temple duties. A Samaritan was considered a half-breed with foreign blood, hated and not worthy of attention by any Jew. Now you are ready for the story. Read it in Luke 10:25-37.

ASK

How well do you know the people who live next door to you?

DISCUSS, BY THE NUMBERS

1. The lawyer thought that he was keeping the Ten Commandments and therefore would get eternal life in heaven. He asked questions to trick Jesus into saying something wrong. Talk about the "whys" of justifying our inappropriate behavior.

2. After your group talks about where they see themselves on the line scale, share your story of how you came to realize your brokenness. The lawyer arrogantly questioned Jesus. Use Proverbs 11:2 and 16:18 to talk about the destructiveness of pride.

3. Listen to your group members' checked responses. Though each of the responses is valid, spend additional time talking about the following statement: Jesus wanted to show that most people have a narrow opinion of who their neighbor is. We want our neighbor to be the people we love. Jesus expanded this definition to include all people, including our enemies.

4. See commentary in bold after each statement.
   - No one today acts like the Samaritan. **Not everyone does, but there still are good Samaritans out there.**
   - You will get sued if you do what the Samaritan did. **While you do have to protect yourself when helping others (liability issues), God's command to love our neighbor has not been rescinded.**
   - The victim was just asking to be robbed by traveling alone; he didn't deserve help. **We often blame victims as an excuse for not helping them.**
   - There is no reward in being a good Samaritan. **The reward may not be earthly, but you will be storing up treasure in heaven for yourself.**
   - I am more like the Samaritan than the priest or Levite. **Good discussion starter. Ask, "What do you think of the Samaritan's actions?"**

5. This situation identifies your neighbor as someone who is not easy to love. Read the situation out loud to your group.

Donnette was so angry. Sara, the girl who sits next to her in Algebra, cheated off her and got caught. Not only did she get her paper taken away, but so did Donnette! Donnette sees Sara crying in the hall. She knows that Sara will probably flunk the class now.

Ask, "What should Donnette say to Sara? Is Sara Donnette's neighbor?"

6. Talk with your group about some of the people that they don't like who are their neighbors and how they can love the unlovable.

THE CLOSE

Read Luke 10:37 out loud. Jesus helped us expand our definition of neighbor. Now we need to "go and do likewise." How we do this will look different for each of us, but we don't want to make excuses or rationalize our selfish behavior any longer. Let's go love our neighbor.

The expert in the law replied, "The one who had mercy on him." Jesus told him, "Go and do likewise." (Luke 10:37)

1. If your house were on fire, what two pieces of stuff would you rush to save?

2. Do you **A (agree)** or **D (disagree)** with each of these statements?

___ Greed can be good.
___ Wanting more stuff is normal.
___ The more stuff you have, the higher your self-esteem.
___ It's bad to want the things others have.
___ You can never have too much stuff.

3. **If you died today, who would get your stuff?**

• My parents
• It would get thrown away
• I don't even want to think about it
• My siblings would fight over it
• It would get sold at a yard sale
• It would be kept in a shrine in my memory
• Other: _____

4. **What is your opinion?**

Good stuff isn't necessarily stuff because—

5. **On the line scale below, place an X to answer the question.**

How does our stuff get in the way of our relationship with Christ?

1	2	3	4	5
Not at all				Totally messes it up

6. **Can a person be wealthy and have a healthy, growing relationship with Christ?**

READ OUT LOUD

Two brothers were fighting over their inheritance. It appears that one of the brothers was greedy, cutting the other brother out of a portion of the inheritance or taking a larger share of the inheritance than he needed. Jesus uses this occasion to teach his disciples about materialism. Read the story found in Luke 12:13-21.

ASK

If you added up the worth of everything on your person right now, how much would it be?

DISCUSS, BY THE NUMBERS

1. Get a faith conversation going on the importance (or lack) of stuff. After listening to your group's answers, ask, "What do the answers have in common?"
2. See commentary in bold after each statement.
   - Greed can be good. **"Greed is good" was the mantra on Wall Street until greed took its toll on the economy. Greed is never good. Greed feeds our self-absorption. We think only of self and neglect the common good of our neighbor.**
   - Wanting more stuff is normal. **It is normal in the sense it is part of our carnal, sinful nature.**
   - The more stuff you have, the higher your self-esteem. **Unfortunately, our net-worth and self-worth are too often connected. We need Christ-esteem rather than self-esteem.**
   - It's bad to want the things that others have. **Yes, this is what the Tenth Commandment is all about.**
   - You can never have too much stuff. **In the United States, most people have too much stuff. Ask, "How much stuff is enough?"**
3. This question gets a good faith conversation going about how unimportant much of our stuff really is.
4. The point of this item is to show that the good life is more about relationships and experiences than the stuff we own.
5. Recreate the line scale on a whiteboard or an easel pad. Ask your group members to place their X on the line. Spend time talking realistically and practically about how materialism gets in the way of your relationship with Christ. It keeps the focus on the unimportant while taking the focus off the important—our relationship with our Savior and Lord.
6. Yes, a person can have great wealth and a growing relationship with Jesus, but it's not easy because of the distracting nature of money.

THE CLOSE

Close by reading Jesus' words from Luke 12:21. Use this closing time to talk about being rich toward God in prayer, Bible reading, faith conversations with friends and family, worship, and other spiritual practices that grow your relationship with Christ. Ask, "How big would your barn have to be to store the love you have for Jesus?"

This is how it will be with those who store up things for themselves but are not rich toward God.
—Jesus, in Luke 12:21

1. The rich man "lived in luxury everyday" (Luke 16:19). This means that the rich man—

- ☐ was guaranteed happiness because he could buy anything he wanted.
- ☐ might have been happy if he bought the right stuff.
- ☐ was miserable because he would have worried about keeping his wealth.

2. **Which one of these statements do you think is most true? The rich man ended up in hell because—**

- ☐ his money was the most important thing in his life
- ☐ you can't be rich and go to heaven
- ☐ his wealth fooled him into thinking he was in control of his life
- ☐ great wealth puts your soul at great risk
- ☐ he was too busy making money to have time for God
- ☐ he put his trust in his wealth rather than in God
- ☐ only poor people make it into heaven
- ☐ he had made up his mind that there was no God, that this world was all there was

3. **The rich man's brothers, according to Jesus, had made up their minds and rejected what the Scripture said about salvation by faith in God. Circle the group of people from the list that are closed-minded about faith in Jesus Christ.**

Atheists   Muslims   Mormons   Agnostics

     Christians   Secular Humanists

4. **Complete this sentence.**

Your spiritual choices matter because—

5. **If you had the wealth of the rich man in the story, what would you do?**

READ OUT LOUD

Today's story is most likely that, a story. It didn't really happen, but is instead a parable that Jesus told, like his many other parables, to make a point. That means the Lazarus talked about in the story was not the Lazarus whom Jesus resurrected. Read the story from Luke 16:19-31.

ASK

What does it mean to have an open mind? To have a closed mind?

DISCUSS, BY THE NUMBERS

1. The point of this item is to get a faith conversation going about happiness. Remember that happiness is determined by external factors, while joy (the kind that Christians experience, anyway) comes from within. One can experience joy no matter what the circumstance.

2. All of the responses could be true. Get your group's opinion regarding each of the statements. You may want to spend some time on the statement, "great wealth puts your soul at great risk," because money and material things can jeopardize your relationship with Christ.

3. Jesus wants us to learn that our life priorities can close our minds to the truth. Talk about each of the groups of people and their level of open-mindedness to the truth of the gospel of Jesus Christ.

   • *Atheists.* Proclaim that there is no God. Leaders in closing their minds to evidence that points to God. Their minds are made up, and no amount of evidence will change their minds.

   • *Muslims.* Believe their prophet Mohammed's proclamation that he alone received the words of the Koran from God. No evidence exists other than Mohammed's word that he told the truth. Open-mindedness looks at the evidence to make a decision. Muslims are willing to die for their beliefs, but they're dying for a belief system rather than solid evidence that their belief system is based on the truth.

   • *Mormons.* Like Muslims rely on Mohammed, Mormons rely on Joseph Smith—the only person to see the tablets on which the book of Mormon was supposedly recorded. Would you want your entire religious system to rely on the word of one man with no witnesses?

   • *Agnostics.* They are not sure about God's existence.

   • *Secular Humanists.* This group believes in the basic goodness of humankind, a falsehood that is easily disputed by looking at the greed and violence of the last century--yet this group continues to close their minds to the sinfulness of humanity.

   • *Christians.* Christians have hundreds of eyewitness accounts of the resurrection. Plus, the disciples, as witnesses to Jesus' death and resurrection, were willing to die for their beliefs. Ask yourself, "Would you die for a belief that you knew was a lie?" This is the most open-minded group on the list because Christians are willing to examine the evidence and base their beliefs on facts, not fantasy or lies. Jesus, in today's story, alluded to his own resurrection in verse 31 when he said, "They will not be convinced even if someone rises from the dead."

4. After listening to the completed sentence stems, start a faith conversation about why spiritual choices matter.

5. See what your group members came up with to answer the question. Ask, "What will you do with the wealth you now have?"

THE CLOSE

Jesus used today's story as a teaching tool to point out that our spiritual decisions do matter. Many people will close their minds to the notion of salvation by faith in Jesus Christ even though the historical evidence points to the truth of this claim. Yet, they will believe in fanciful ideas of aliens bringing life to earth or New Age beliefs. How closed-minded are you? Are you willing to examine the facts of the gospel—that Jesus is who he said he is?

1. **Why do you think someone rich like Zacchaeus would be interested in Jesus?**

   - ❏ Zacchaeus heard that Jesus owed back taxes.
   - ❏ Zacchaeus wanted Jesus to help him grow taller—something his money couldn't buy him.
   - ❏ Zacchaeus wanted someone to like him for something other than his money and hoped Jesus would be that friend.
   - ❏ Zacchaeus was searching for a bigger purpose in his life—his wealth had not given him true joy.
   - ❏ Zacchaeus was into climbing trees and just happened to see Jesus.

2. **Zacchaeus' family was ready to receive Jesus into their home. If Jesus came to your home, what would he see?**

   a. Me—yelling at my mom or dad.
   b. Me—fighting with my brother or sister.
   c. Me—saying I was sorry when I hurt another family member.
   d. Me—trying to get away with as much as I could.
   e. Me—pitching a fit when I don't get something I want.

3. **What can we learn from Zacchaeus' encounter with Jesus?**

   - ❏ Jesus wants us to seek him out.
   - ❏ Climbing a tree gets you saved.
   - ❏ Jesus is more interested in the condition of your heart than how much or little money you have.
   - ❏ Zacchaeus was the scum of the earth, and so am I.
   - ❏ Jesus is in the salvation business.
   - ❏ Jesus only stayed in nice homes.
   - ❏ Wealthy people also need Jesus.

4. **Which of the following statements are T (true) and which are F (false)?**

   ___ If Jesus wanted to be popular, he shouldn't have talked to Zacchaeus.
   ___ The Jews' hatred of Zacchaeus was justified.
   ___ The Jews would have been surprised by Jesus' response to seeing Zacchaeus in the tree.
   ___ Zacchaeus didn't deserve the forgiveness of his horrible sins. He robbed the people of what little money they had through exorbitant taxes.
   ___ Jesus was reluctant to forgive Zacchaeus.

5. **How would you finish this statement?**
   Zacchaeus showed that he had repented of his sins by—

6. **Jesus "came to seek and to save what was lost" (Luke 19:10).** How was Zacchaeus an example of the "lost"? How are you an example?

READ OUT LOUD

The Jews considered Zacchaeus the "scum of the earth" because he was in charge of the tax collectors. They ripped off the people, collecting more than necessary for their Roman bosses. Keeping people poor while lining his pockets with money was something Zacchaeus had done for years. And if anyone refused, he had the power of the Roman army to back him up. The leaders of the Roman Empire cared little for their subjects unless they were valid Roman citizens. Now let's look at Luke 19:1-10.

ASK

Who would you consider to be the scum of the earth?

DISCUSS, BY THE NUMBERS

1. Have fun with each of the responses. Focus your attention on, "Zacchaeus was searching for a bigger purpose in his life—his wealth had not given him true joy." Ask, "How is this like people you know?"

2. Response "c" is how a Christian would act at home. Ask, "What would your parent or stepparent tell Jesus about you?"

3. Talk about the checked responses found below. Commentary can be found in bold after each of the statements.
   - Jesus wants us to seek him out. **The Lord welcomes anyone seeking him with open arms.**
   - Jesus is more interested in the condition of your heart than how much or little money you have. **Jesus saw the condition of Zacchaeus' heart, a person seeking to know more about him.**
   - Zacchaeus was the scum of the earth, and so am I. **Everyone is a sinner—the scum of the earth. When you recognize you are the scum of the earth and repent as Zacchaeus did, then you are saved.**
   - Jesus is in the salvation business. **He came to save the lost as today's story reminds us.**
   - Wealthy people also need Jesus. **Everyone needs Jesus.**

4. See commentary in bold after each statement.
   - If Jesus wanted to be popular, he shouldn't have talked to Zacchaeus. **Since Zacchaeus was so hated because of his job, Jesus didn't win any new friends by going to his home.**
   - The Jews' hatred of Zacchaeus was justified. **His treatment of his fellow Jews had been reprehensible, yet he sought forgiveness—something they did not want to extend to him. They were guilty of not loving their neighbor. Ask, "How often do you love your enemies?"**
   - The Jews would have been surprised by Jesus' response to seeing Zacchaeus in the tree. **True. It was getting close to the time that Jesus would triumphantly enter Jerusalem (we call it Palm Sunday today). The Jews following after Jesus were expecting him to overthrow the Roman Empire, not befriend Zacchaeus, a supporter of Roman rule and power.**
   - Zacchaeus didn't deserve the forgiveness of his horrible sins. **He robbed the people of what little money they had through exorbitant taxes. True, nobody deserves God's grace. That's why it is a free gift.**
   - Jesus was reluctant to forgive Zacchaeus. **Never. Jesus welcomes everyone to repent of their sins and freely forgives.**

5. The answer? Zacchaeus showed a repentant heart by paying back the money he had stolen. Ask, "Have you proved that you have a repentant heart?"

6. Listen to your group's answers. Describe how you were lost and then found by Jesus.

THE CLOSE

In God's eyes we are the scum of the earth, just like Zacchaeus, until we repent and turn our lives over to Jesus Christ. Our sins are no different than Zacchaeus'. Those without Christ often compare their sins to those of others and think they come out of the comparison okay. From their perspective they don't need Jesus or any sort of salvation from sin because they are okay. Their good outweighs their bad. But when you compare your sins to God's standard of holiness, you are, in fact, scum of the earth and in desperate need of a Savior.

A DISAPPOINTED RICH GUY

Nothing should stand between Jesus and us

1. **The rich guy thought, as many people do today, that you had to be good enough; you had to earn eternal life with God.**

• I have definitely believed, like the rich guy, that I had to earn my way to heaven.
• I have sometimes believed I needed to be good enough to get into heaven.
• I have never believed that my good works would get me into heaven.

2. **Jesus mentions God's commands that relate to relationships with others.**

   "You shall not murder." (Exodus 20:13)
   "You shall not commit adultery." (Exodus 20:14)
   "You shall not steal." (Exodus 20:15)
   "You shall not give false testimony against your neighbor." (Exodus 20:16)
   "Honor your father and your mother…" (Exodus 20:12)
   "…love your neighbor as yourself." (Leviticus 19:18)

   Why do you think Jesus left out the first four commands that focus on our relationship with God?

3. **What do you think the rich guy meant when he said, "All these have I kept"?**

   • that he had never, ever sinned.
   • that he had tried really, really hard to keep God's commandments.
   • that he had paid attention to God's commandments and obeyed when he could.
   • that he had not obeyed them but was lying to Jesus.

4. **After telling Jesus that he had kept the commandments Jesus mentioned, the rich guy asked, "What do I still lack?"**

   I think his conscience bothered him because—

5. **The one thing that stood between the rich guy and God was his money. Is there anything in your life that keeps you from devoting yourself fully to Christ?**

6. **Which of these statements do you think are true?**

   ___ Rich people are blessed by God.
   ___ You can trust Christ and your wealth at the same time.
   ___ Rich people are those who are billionaires.
   ___ Poor people have as hard a time as the wealthy getting into heaven.
   ___ It's better to be rich than to be poor.

READ OUT LOUD

Mark 10:17 tells us that a wealthy man came running to Jesus, humbly knelt down, and asked the most important question anyone could ask. This rich guy was searching for the truth. Something was missing from his life that his wealth could not purchase. You can read the story from Matthew 19:16-23.

ASK

How wealthy do you think you will be?

DISCUSS, BY THE NUMBERS

1. Use this item to talk about the persistent belief that people must and can earn their way to heaven. So many religions hold this tenet as part of their beliefs (Mormons, Jehovah's Witnesses, Muslims, Hindus, and more). Jesus had to correct the thinking of the rich guy. This is why Jesus says that only God is good—because humankind can never be good enough to have a right relationship with God.

2. Jesus lists those commands that relate to relationships with others. He seems to have substituted Leviticus 19:18 (love for neighbor) for the Tenth Commandment (don't want things that belong to your neighbor). Jesus skips the first four of the Ten Commandments, which relate to our relationship with God, most likely because these were the ones the man was not keeping. His wealth seemed to have stood between him and God.

3. The rich guy probably meant that he had paid attention to God's commandments and obeyed when he could. He was doing the best that any human could do.

4. The rich guy knew something was lacking in his life. His conscience told him that he had missed something. Listen to what your group members thought his conscience was telling him. A blind spot for the man was his love of his wealth. This was the one thing that was keeping him from a right relationship with God.

5. Create a list of responses to the question, "Is there anything in your life that keeps you from devoting yourself fully to Christ?"

6. See commentary in bold after each statement.
   - God blesses rich people. **Their riches are proof that God blesses them. This was a mistaken theology of the Jews.**
   - You can trust Christ and your wealth at the same time. **Jesus told us that you can't serve God and money (Matthew 6:24).**
   - Rich people are only those who are billionaires. **Debate what makes someone monetarily rich.**
   - Poor people have as hard a time as the wealthy getting into heaven. **The poor have an advantage in that they don't have wealth to rely on instead of God. But a poor person can still trust in himself rather than God, and so have a hard time finding the humility that is needed to accept Christ as Savior.**
   - It's better to be rich than to be poor. **Proverbs 30:8 tells us that being neither rich nor poor is a good thing. The writer of the Proverb, Agur, says, "Give me neither poverty nor riches, but give me only my daily bread."**

THE CLOSE

The rich guy walked away from Jesus deeply disappointed and sad because he was too attached to his wealth. All that money got in the way of his relationship with God. Let's examine our lives. Let's see what barriers there are that block our relationship with Christ. And let's remove those barriers so that nothing stands in the way between Jesus and us.

1. Martha enthusiastically welcomed Jesus into her home. How enthusiastic are you about opening your home life to Jesus?

- ☐ I live in a home with at least one Christian parent. Christ is welcomed in my home and seen in my life at home.
- ☐ I live in a home with at least one Christian parent. Christ is welcomed in my home but not often seen in my life at home.
- ☐ I live in a home with no Christian parent. Christ is seen in my life at home.
- ☐ I live in a home with no Christian parent. Christ is not seen in my life at home.

21. Luke 10:38-42

MARY & MARTHA

Let's keep the main thing the main thing, and that's Jesus

2. Sitting at the feet of Jesus means that Mary was a disciple of his. She enthusiastically wanted to learn from Jesus about living a godly life. Respond with a Y (yes) or N (no) to each of the following statements.

- ___ I'm an enthusiastic follower of Christ.
- ___ It's not popular to be an enthusiastic follower of Christ.
- ___ My friends are as enthusiastic as I am about following Christ.
- ___ My church is filled with enthusiastic followers of Christ.
- ___ I know adults outside my church who are enthusiastic followers of Christ.

3. What do you think—do you A (agree) or D (disagree)?

- ___ Martha worried too much.
- ___ It was a good thing for Martha to want to be a good hostess to Jesus and the disciples.
- ___ Martha made a mistake in telling Jesus to get Mary to help her.
- ___ The disciples should have pitched in and helped Martha with the food and other preparations for Jesus' stay.
- ___ Martha was not a follower of Jesus.

4. "You are worried and upset about many things" (Luke 10:41) was how Jesus answered Martha's question. She had become distracted from the truly important things in life. If Jesus said this to you, what do you think he would see distracting you?

5. Rank the following relationships from 1 (least important) to 10 (most important).

- ___ Christ
- ___ My mom
- ___ My schoolwork
- ___ My best friend
- ___ My dad

- ___ My sport(s)
- ___ My brother/sister
- ___ My music
- ___ My church
- ___ My job

READ OUT LOUD

Martha, most likely a widow, lived with her brother, Lazarus, and her sister, Mary. Jesus loved the three of them (John 11:5) and decided to stay at their home. It seems the home belonged to Martha, left to her by her late husband. Read the story found in Luke 10:38-42.

ASK

Who does most of the work around your house when friends come to visit?

DISCUSS, BY THE NUMBERS

1. See commentary in bold after each statement.
   - I live in a home with at least one Christian parent. Christ is welcomed in my home and seen in my life at home. **Possibly vibrant Christian home where the family talks often about Christ. Talk about the importance of faith conversation in the home.**
   - I live in a home with at least one Christian parent. Christ is welcomed in my home but not often seen in my life at home. **Young person not living the Christian life at home. Parent may or may not be living like Christ at home. Ask, "Why would it be important to live like Christ at home?"**
   - I live in a home with no Christian parent. Christ is seen in my life at home. **Young person is a witness at home. Ask, "What happens when there is a witness in a home without a Christian parent?"**
   - I live in a home with no Christian parent. Christ is not often seen in my life at home. **Young person is not a witness at home. Talk about the need for a Christian witness in this home even though it is difficult.**
2. See commentary in bold after each statement.
   - I'm an enthusiastic follower of Christ. **Ask, "What does this look like?"**
   - It is not popular to be an enthusiastic follower of Christ. **Often, one is put down as a fanatic. It's good to be a fan of Jesus though.**
   - My friends are as enthusiastic as I am about following Christ. **Having friends who share your Christian values helps. Ask, "How can you encourage your friends to enthusiastically follow Christ?"**
   - My church is filled with enthusiastic followers of Christ. **Not always true, unfortunately. Talk about how the enthusiasm of the young people in your congregation can spread like a virus.**

- I know adults outside my church who are enthusiastic followers of Christ. **It is necessary to have adult role models for enthusiasm to last.**

3. See commentary in bold after each statement.
   - Martha worried too much. **This can be one to debate with your group.**
   - It was a good thing for Martha to want to be a good hostess to Jesus and the disciples. **In her defense, Martha wanted to make a good impression on Christ. She wanted to make sure the meal and refreshments were ready on time.**
   - Martha made a mistake in telling Jesus to get Mary to help her. **Probably, there was some sibling rivalry going on here. It is this rivalry playing out that Jesus saw in the question Martha asked him.**
   - The disciples should have pitched in and helped Martha with the food and other preparations for Jesus' stay. **In the culture of that day, domestic chores were taken care of by women, who were seen as "less than." It is amazing that Jesus allowed Mary to sit at his feet as a disciple—something reserved for men only. Jesus elevated women's status through his friendship with women and his teachings. Christianity elevated the role of women as it spread through the Western world. Observe how women are treated where Christianity is not prevalent (Muslim countries, for example).**
   - Martha was not a follower of Jesus. **She was a follower, but she was distracted at this time from the more important task of spending time with Christ.**

4. Together, as a group, answer the question, "What do you think Jesus sees distracting you in your relationship with him?" Make a list of distractions. Then talk about strategies for overcoming these distractions.

5. The Sunday school answer ranks Christ as number one. Ask the group to honestly assess their relationships. Then talk about how to make and keep Christ as number one.

THE CLOSE

The things of this world can become easy distractions that keep us away from Jesus. We need to daily examine our life priorities if we are to keep Christ number one. [Tell a story of how you have failed to do this and what did or will get you back on track. Don't be afraid to let your group members know that you have failed at consistently keeping Christ in the number-one-priority slot.]

JESUS PREACHES WHILE HE HEALS

Does telling others of Jesus' love include meeting their physical needs?

1. How often do you pray in private as Jesus did?

- ☐ All the time
- ☐ Now and then
- ☐ Fairly regularly
- ☐ Never

2. Jesus traveled through the towns of Galilee sharing the good news. Where are you willing to go to tell others of Jesus' love?

- ☐ Anywhere in my neighborhood
- ☐ Anywhere in my hometown
- ☐ Anywhere in North America
- ☐ Anywhere in Central or South America
- ☐ Anywhere in Asia
- ☐ Anywhere in Europe
- ☐ Anywhere in the Caribbean
- ☐ Anywhere in Australia
- ☐ Anywhere in Africa
- ☐ Anywhere

3. If I were in the crowd listening to Jesus I would have wanted to hear him say—

4. Respond to each of the following statements with a Y (yes), N (no), or MS (maybe so).

___ Jesus was tricked by the man with leprosy into healing him.

___ Jesus hurt when he saw someone suffering from leprosy, blindness, or other disabilities.

___ Jesus healed many more people than the four Gospels record.

___ Jesus demonstrated on the spot his infinite compassion and love for humankind through his healing ministry.

___ Jesus could not have healed anyone he wanted.

5. What do you think Jesus' curing the sick, healing the disabled, and feeding the hungry had to do with the good news?

READ OUT LOUD

Jesus had been healing people of a variety of diseases in the days before this story unfolded. He awoke early to find an isolated spot in which to pray. Read the story found in Mark 1:35-45.

ASK

What is the sickest you've ever been?

DISCUSS, BY THE NUMBERS

1. Identify which of the four was checked the most. Ask, "Why weren't the disciples up early praying with Jesus? How important is it to get alone when you pray?"

2. Jesus was willing to diligently pursue his mission of sharing the good news with as many communities as he could reach in Palestine. Use this item to talk about the places your group members are willing to go to tell others of Jesus' love. And ask why it is important to go to places other than where you live.

3. Listen to your group members' responses to the sentence stem. Talk about the content of the good news: 1) Awareness of brokenness—there is evil in the world and in us; 2) We can't fix that brokenness on our own; 3) We must repent; 4) We must turn our lives over to Jesus Christ by faith that he can fix us.

4. See commentary in bold after each statement.
   - Jesus was tricked by the man with leprosy into healing him. **Disagree. The man suffering from leprosy begged Jesus for healing, saying, "If you are willing, you can make me clean." (Mark 1:40) The man asked to be healed and Jesus said yes.**
   - Jesus hurt when he saw someone suffering from leprosy, blindness, or other disabilities. **Agree. Christ was filled with compassion. His healing ministry was not only evidence of his divinity but of his infinite love for humankind.**
   - Jesus healed many more people than the four Gospels record. **John 20:30-31 says only a portion of his miracles are recorded in the Bible.**
   - Jesus demonstrated on the spot his infinite compassion and love for humankind through his healing ministry. **Right then and there Jesus showed his love for humankind and, ultimately, his infinite love for us was shown through his death on the cross.**
   - Jesus could not have healed anyone he wanted. **Yes, he could have but chose not to because this was not part of God's bigger plan of salvation.**

5. There are some Christians who want to separate Jesus' feeding of the hungry, teaching about justice for the poor, curing the sick, or healing the disabled from his preaching of the good news. Its critics sometimes call this approach "hit and run evangelism" because it focuses only on people's souls apart from their needs. The Bible teaches that Jesus tied his preaching of the gospel to taking care of people's physical needs. We can do the same when it is appropriate.

THE CLOSE

Jesus wants us to share the gospel, as he did, with the lost. As we share we are commanded to also care about social justice, about poverty and hunger, about those who are homeless, about those addicted to alcohol and other drugs. What kind of love does it show when we share God's love and let the people with whom we share continue in their hunger or homelessness?

Note: Old Testament law required those healed of leprosy check in with the priest to verify the cure. Why? To protect the public against a fake cure. In today's account of healing, Jesus wanted the healed man to keep the law, so he told him to go see the priest. Jesus may have had an additional reason for sending the man to be checked by the priest—to verify the healing by Christ as a genuine miracle.

1. **You can put your faith in Jesus Christ and believe in reincarnation.**

   - ☐ I strongly agree.
   - ☐ I agree.
   - ☐ I don't know.
   - ☐ I disagree.
   - ☐ I strongly disagree.

BELIEFS ABOUT A HEALING

What you believe really does matter

2. **Each of the following statements represents a belief taken from the "transmigration of the soul" belief system. Read the belief statement, then answer the question with a Yes or a No, as if you held that belief yourself.**

   - You could sin while still in your mother's womb. Does that mean your blindness could be your fault? ☐ Yes ☐ No

   - If you were born poor, you were being punished for egregious sins from a previous life. Does that mean you should stay poor your entire life? ☐ Yes ☐ No

   - You may have to pay for the sins of your parents. Does that mean your misfortune may be your parents' fault? ☐ Yes ☐ No

3. **Respond to these statements with a Y (yes), N (no), or MS (maybe so).**

   ___ To get into heaven, it doesn't matter what you believe as long as you sincerely believe something.
   ___ You'll live your life differently if you believe in the Golden Rule than if you don't believe in it.
   ___ Our thoughts and behaviors have consequences beyond us.
   ___ Loving your neighbor is as important as loving yourself.
   ___ Money and pleasure are the keys to well-being.
   ___ Putting your faith in Christ is the only way to get your sins forgiven.
   ___ God desires that everyone should put their trust in Jesus.
   ___ The Muslim belief that you must work your way into heaven could be right.
   ___ There's more than one correct religion.
   ___ There could be many gods (like the Romans and Greeks believed).

4. **Jesus showed compassion to the blind guy. How can you show compassion to those with disabilities?**

5. **If you have questions about what you believe, with whom could you talk?**

6. **The Old Testament prophet Isaiah predicted that the coming Messiah would heal the blind; thus, in doing the miraculous healing of the man born blind, Jesus was proving that he was the Savior. Why do you think many in Israel still did not believe in Jesus as the Messiah? Why do you think you do believe in Jesus as the Messiah?**

READ OUT LOUD

The transmigration of the soul is a belief that has persisted for thousands of years. This belief system simply states is that one's soul is born into a new body for punishment of sins previously committed in one's old body. Hindus today believe a version of this called reincarnation. The disciples were alluding to this belief system when they asked if the man blind from birth was being punished for sins committed in a pre-existing state or for the sins of his parents. This false belief system affected their doctrine of sin. Read the story found in John 9:1-12.

ASK

How many of your friends do you think believe in reincarnation?

DISCUSS, BY THE NUMBERS

1. The problem, it has been said, with Americans is not that they don't believe in anything but that they believe everything. This item is a great one to debate. Can you truly be a believer in Jesus Christ and also believe in reincarnation? The two belief systems certainly contradict each other, and Jesus, in today's story, tells the disciples that reincarnation is not the reason the man was born blind.

2. A belief system colors how one sees the world, makes decisions, and acts. See the commentary in bold after each of the belief statements.

   - You could sin while still in your mother's womb. Does that mean your blindness could be your fault? **Yes, if you believed in the transmigration of the soul, then you would believe that sin before birth was possible, and thus blindness was caused by your sin. You can begin to see how your beliefs affect your thoughts and your actions.**

   - If you were born poor, you were being punished for egregious sins from a previous life. Does that mean you should stay poor your entire life? **Yes. That's why those in the lowest caste in India are poor and must stay poor. They are paying for their sins committed in a previous life. Did you see the movie *Slumdog Millionaire*? Some Indians were upset with the movie because the young man, born into the lower caste, was not supposed to win the million dollars.**

   - You may have to pay for the sins of your parents. Does that mean your misfortune may be your parents' fault? **Yes, the belief was parents would have to watch their child suffer for their sins. The Bible is clear—suffering is not always because of personal sin. Sin does produce consequences in which the sinner suffers, but not all suffering results from sin. When you believe that suffering is always produced by your sin, then your belief system is leading you astray. What you believe does matter.**

3. See commentary in bold after each statement.

   - To get into heaven, it doesn't matter what you believe as long as you sincerely believe something. **No way. What we believe does matter. Different religions have beliefs that contradict Christianity. They all can't be**

correct. Yet, in today's culture of relative morality, it isn't politically correct to evaluate the truth claims of different belief systems. We are to "appreciate" all belief systems as equally valid.

   - You'll live your life differently if you believe in the Golden Rule than if you don't believe in it. **The Golden Rule—treat others the way you want to be treated. Let's say you don't believe in the Golden Rule but believe, "Rip off others before they rip you off." That belief will affect the way you behave, and you will behave badly.**

   - Our thoughts and behaviors have consequences beyond us. **Yes they do. That's again why what you believe matters.**

   - Loving your neighbor is as important as loving yourself. **As with the Golden Rule, if you believe this, then you will act differently than if you don't.**

   - Money and pleasure are the keys to well-being. **Many people believe this and make life goals and decisions based on this belief, only to be disappointed because the belief is invalid.**

   - Putting your faith in Christ is the only way to get your sins forgiven. **True, so this belief affects you for eternity.**

   - God desires that all people should put their trust in Jesus. **Yes, and this belief should affect who you talk to about Jesus.**

   - The Muslim belief that you must work your way into heaven could be right. **No, but this belief is fooling a billion people into thinking they may go to heaven.**

   - There's more than one correct religion. **No. Only one can be correct. This has been called the "problem of exclusivity" because people are upset that Christians believe Jesus is the only way.**

   - There could be many gods (like the Romans and Greeks believed). **This belief system fooled the ancient Romans and Greeks and is today fooling millions of Hindus.**

4. Make a list of the ways in which your group members can show the compassion of Jesus to those with disabilities.

5. Discuss the kinds of people your group members could go to with their belief questions. Also talk about the importance of regular Bible study with others as a way to sharpen your Christian belief system.

6. Discuss the group's answers to the two questions. The Isaiah verses can be found in Isaiah 29:18, 35:5, and 42:7.

THE CLOSE

What you believe really does matter. Our beliefs color our thinking and, consequently, our actions. When people believed that the world was flat, they were afraid to sail too far out to sea because they thought they would fall off the edge. When people believe in reincarnation, then they can easily believe that the poor deserve what they get because of their sins in previous existences. Knowing what the truth is also matters because you want to believe in the truth. If Jesus really is God and he really did die and come back to life to save sinful humanity, then we'd better believe it, and that belief ought to change the way we live.

24. John 5:1-15

THE HEALING AT THE POOL

What stands in the way of Jesus working in your life?

1. The man's fear kept him from taking a risk and plunging alone into the healing pool. What fears keep you from allowing Jesus to work more fully in your life?

- ☐ I'm afraid I'll lose some of my friends.
- ☐ I'm afraid people will make fun of me.
- ☐ I won't be considered cool any longer.
- ☐ I'll have to stop doing things I want to do.
- ☐ God will send me to Africa as a missionary.

2. The disabled man never asked Jesus for help. Jesus chose to help the man even though the man seemed to lack the faith necessary for Jesus to work in his life. How does this give you hope? Circle the one statement that gives you the most hope.

   a. There are times when I forget to ask God for help.
   b. It shows that God is compassionate, the kind of God I want to serve.
   c. God still cares and will help me even when I don't do life right.
   d. It's good to know that Jesus wants to help me.
   e. I know I have a God who is there for me no matter what.

3. The disabled man, carrying his mat on the Sabbath, was a problem for many of the more traditional Jews. This was a misinterpretation of God's command to rest on the Sabbath. What man-made rules keep you from letting Jesus work in your life?

- ☐ *The busier you are, the better.*
- ☐ *Your net worth (how much you have) determines your self-worth.*
- ☐ *The most important thing in life is family.*
- ☐ *You don't need anyone else but yourself to succeed.*
- ☐ *You have to work hard to make anything of yourself.*

4. Why do you think the man healed of his disability would not try to find out more about Jesus, the person who healed him? How are you ignoring your relationship with Christ?

5. The man Christ healed of the disability knew nothing about Jesus. How could you get to know Jesus better? Rank the following from 1 (the best way) to 7 (the worst way) to get to know Christ better.

   ___ Pray regularly every day.
   ___ Watch the History Channel.
   ___ Read a book about growing closer to Jesus.
   ___ Find a trustworthy person to mentor you in your relationship with Christ.
   ___ Read one of the four books called the Gospels—Matthew, Mark, Luke, or John.
   ___ Watch a movie about the life of Christ.
   ___ Join a small group Bible study that meets regularly.

6. Jesus told the man he healed that the consequences of his sins, both eternal and temporary on earth, were much worse than any disability. Do you think the man took Jesus seriously, repented of his sins, and put his faith in Christ? How could your sins keep Christ from working in your life?

READ OUT LOUD

For a long time, 38 years to be exact, a man lay out in the dirt and rock, afraid to get into a healing pool by himself. The disabled man's fear stood in the way of his healing until Jesus intervened. Biblical archaeologists in Israel have located this healing pool. Tradition had it that once each year an angel would "stir up" the waters, resulting in their curative properties. Read John 5:1-14 out loud to learn more.

ASK

What is your biggest fear?

DISCUSS, BY THE NUMBERS

1. Fear stands in the way of people allowing Jesus to work more fully in their lives. Let your group members identify the things they fear happening that keep them from being 100 percent committed to Christ. The disabled man's fear kept him from taking a risk and plunging alone into the healing pool. Perhaps he was afraid of drowning. Maybe he didn't really believe that healing by God in the pool was possible. Whatever he feared, the man lay by the pool for 38 long years begging for a living and hoping for help.

2. Look at the most popular reason for hope. Say, "God is a gracious God. We need not do everything right for him to work in our lives." Ask, "What do you think Jesus wants to do in your life? How strong is your desire for God to work in your life? When do you think you will be willing to take a risk and let God work in you?"

3. Like the Pharisees and other outwardly religious Jews of Jesus' time, we too have man-made rules that keep us from letting Jesus work in our lives. Choose the most popular one out of the five (or think of another one) and talk about why it is a roadblock to Jesus working in the lives of your group members.

4. Why do you think the man healed of his disability would *not* try to find out more about Jesus, the person who healed him? We do it all the time—neglecting to thank God for answered prayer; watching Christ work in our lives, then worrying; forgetting the great things we have seen God do in the lives of others. Start a faith conversation on how we can often ignore our relationship with Christ.

5. After listening to two of the rank orders of your group members, see if you can rank the seven as a group. Ask your group members to commit to one of the ideas.

6. Jesus showed concern in verse 14 for more than just the man's physical health. He wanted the man to repent and put his faith in him. While Jesus demonstrated compassion for people's physical needs, he knew that the spiritual realm was far more important.

THE CLOSE

What stands in the way of Jesus working in your life? Are you afraid of what others might think if you are 100 percent sold out to Jesus? Are you worried that you might lose your friends? Are you apprehensive that God might send you to a Muslim country as a missionary? We need not let fear stand in the way of letting Jesus work in our lives. We stand to gain so much more, both in eternity as well as in the here and now, by letting Jesus have 100 percent of us.

CHRIST RIDES HUMBLY TO THE RESCUE

Look to Jesus to come to your rescue

1. Jesus' ride into Jerusalem has been called "The Triumphal Entry." What does triumph mean? How was the ride of Jesus a triumph?

2. The disciples, by laying their clothing on the donkey, announced that Jesus was their King and Savior. How do you announce that Jesus is your Savior? (Pick your top two.)

- ☐ Wear Christian T-shirts
- ☐ Say, "God bless you," when someone sneezes
- ☐ Carry my Bible at school
- ☐ Listen to Christian music
- ☐ Talk with others about Christ
- ☐ Wear a cross necklace
- ☐ Pray before I eat lunch
- ☐ Act like I'm a Christian
- ☐ Invite my friends to church
- ☐ Put a Christian bumper sticker on my or my family's car

The clothing placed on the donkey was the way the disciples announced that Jesus was their King and Savior. Where do you stand? Check the one that fits you the best.

- ☐ I tell everyone I know that Jesus is my Savior.
- ☐ Most of my friends know that Jesus is my Savior.
- ☐ Some of my friends know that Jesus is my Savior.
- ☐ A few people know that Jesus is my Savior.
- ☐ I hide the fact that Jesus is my Savior.

3. Do you A (agree) or D (disagree)?

___ The crowd thought, after all his miracles, that Jesus could conquer the Romans.
___ The crowd was ready for Jesus to take power by force.
___ The crowd honoring Christ was clueless about the Old Testament prophecies concerning Jesus.
___ The crowd was sick and tired of being sick and tired.
___ The crowd wanted more miracles.

4. The people of Jerusalem were excited about Jesus' arrival as their Messiah. Why do you think five days later they wanted to crucify him?

- ☐ It was very strange.
- ☐ People often can make stupid decisions they later regret.
- ☐ They got it right, then they got it wrong.
- ☐ We do the same thing today by one day making Jesus our Lord and the next ignoring him.

5. Has Jesus ridden into town and rescued you?

- ☐ I don't need to be rescued.
- ☐ I know I need rescuing, but not yet.
- ☐ I see the cosmic Jesus as the energy force of the universe that binds me to all other living things.
- ☐ Jesus is the rescuer for me, but other religions have their own ways of rescue.
- ☐ Jesus is my one and only hope to have a right relationship with God.

READ OUT LOUD

The triumphal entry was popular in Roman times. A military leader would be paraded into a city as a ceremonial honor of his victory. Jesus' ride into Jerusalem fulfilled another Old Testament prediction about him as Messiah (Zechariah 9:9). The ride symbolized Jesus' coming victory over sin. The people laid clothing and palm branches in the road to honor Christ. They shouted *Hosanna*, which means, "to save now." They saw Jesus as the Messiah riding into Jerusalem to rescue them from the oppression of the Romans. The story can be read from Matthew 21:1-11.

ASK

When you enter a room, would you rather come in quietly or have everybody look at you?

DISCUSS, BY THE NUMBERS

1. Talk about how Jesus' ride into Jerusalem was a triumph of humility over pride, good over evil, poverty over wealth, compassion over indifference, or peace over power.
2. You can go back to 2 Kings 9:13 to see the Jewish tradition of spreading clothing out to announce a king. Each of the 10 statements is a way to announce that you are a Christian. Talk about the pluses and minuses of each.
3. See commentary in bold after each statement.
   - The crowd thought, after all his miracles, that Jesus could conquer the Romans. **They misread the role of the Messiah in their hope to have a conqueror of their Roman oppressors.**
   - The crowd was ready for Jesus to take power by force. **They saw brute force as the only way to overcome their Roman oppressors. Jesus' upside-down kingdom, even though they heard him preach it, was foreign to them.**
   - The crowd honoring Christ was clueless about the Old Testament prophecies concerning Jesus. **Probably not totally clueless, for they knew that a Messiah was coming.**
   - The crowd was sick and tired of being sick and tired. **Yes, they were tired of being ruled by the Romans.**
   - The crowd wanted more miracles. **Probably!**
4. They certainly got it right on Palm Sunday but got it wrong by Friday. We often do the same today by making Jesus Lord one day and ignoring him the next.
5. See commentary in bold after each statement.
   - I don't need to be rescued. **Everyone needs it, but not everyone knows they need it. Some people think they can do fine being in charge of their own lives.**
   - I know I need rescuing, but not yet. **Some of us want salvation—later, but not now; this is a mistake because you miss out on all the blessings of the Christian life.**
   - I see the cosmic Jesus as the energy force of the universe that binds me to all other living things. **A New-Age belief.**
   - Jesus is the rescuer for me, but other religions have their own ways of rescue. **This statement sees that all religions lead to the same place.**
   - Jesus is my one and only hope to have a right relationship with God. **Yes!**

THE CLOSE

The people of Jerusalem wanted someone to take out their Roman oppressors. Christ was their guy. But in five days they took him out. We have the perspective of looking back and seeing the resurrection and knowing that, yes, Jesus is our Savior. We can shout *Hosanna* and know what it really means—that Jesus is the way, the truth, and the life!

1. The salespeople in the temple were all about making money rather than about worshiping God. Theirs was a pretend faith. Why do you think people pretend to be Christians today? (Check the top three.)

- ☐ To please their parents
- ☐ To make business contacts among Christians
- ☐ Because they were raised in a church
- ☐ To use Christians to get ahead in life
- ☐ To make money off the church
- ☐ Because everybody else does it
- ☐ To find people to date
- ☐ Because they think it will help them get into heaven
- ☐ So people will trust them in business
- ☐ Other: _____

26. Matthew 21:12-15

JESUS CHASES OUT THE SALESPEOPLE FROM THE TEMPLE

Dedicate a place where you can be alone with God

2. The temple was a place dedicated to making things right with God. How does a person make his or her life right with God today?

- ☐ Do more good than bad.
- ☐ Go to church on Easter and Christmas.
- ☐ Put money in the offering plate.
- ☐ Act religious.
- ☐ Put your faith in Christ.
- ☐ Give to TV evangelists.
- ☐ Join a church.
- ☐ Pray to the Universe.
- ☐ Live the Golden Rule.
- ☐ Worship the god of a religion.
- ☐ Pray before you go to bed.
- ☐ Obey the Ten Commandments.

3. People prayed while they were at the temple. What place or places could you dedicate to spending time alone with God?

4. The temple is no longer the place where God hangs out. God now chooses to dwell in each Christian by the presence of the Holy Spirit. What is one character flaw that you would like Christ to clean up in you?

- ☐ Lack of patience
- ☐ Anger problem
- ☐ Love of money
- ☐ Jealousy
- ☐ Disrespect
- ☐ Dishonesty
- ☐ Other: _____
- ☐ Laziness
- ☐ Lack of self-control
- ☐ Lack of commitment
- ☐ Lack of compassion
- ☐ Rebelliousness
- ☐ Lust for things I can't have

5. Those suffering from disabilities came to Jesus in the outer courtyard of the temple to be healed. How often do you pray for the healing of others?

READ OUT LOUD

There was a space within the outer walls of the temple where people bought and sold sacrificial animals that were used to meet God's law for forgiveness of sins. Jesus drives them out of this space. You can read the story found in Matthew 21:12-15.

ASK

How long does it take you to clean your room?

DISCUSS, BY THE NUMBERS

1. This item can start a faith conversation on authentically living for Christ rather than pretending or going through the motions. Talk about the advantages of following Jesus enthusiastically.

2. The only way to make things right with God is through repentance—admitting your brokenness and putting your faith in Christ. The other things aren't bad (except for praying to the Universe—a New Age concept—acting religious, and arguably giving to TV evangelists) but won't make you right with God.

3. Talk about the helpfulness of a dedicated place to pray—those one or two places you and God can get together for some one-on-one time without distractions.

4. See if there are one or two common issues that need a cleaning job by Christ.

5. After clearing out the temple courtyard, Jesus showed the people one of the ministries that needed to occur there. Have a conversation about the ministry of prayer for others who are sick, disabled, and hurting rather than just praying for your own needs.

THE CLOSE

Jesus is moving toward the cross. Before he gets there, though, he cleans up the temple. He wanted the people to know that the temple was dedicated for special service to God. And like the temple of old, our bodies are the place where the Holy Spirit lives. We need to dedicate our bodies, our minds, and our spirits to serving Christ. This means that we need a daily check of our condition to ensure that nothing is in us that could block the work of the Holy Spirit through us.

1. The cursing of the fig tree symbolized judgment. Jesus used the fig tree to show that judgment was coming. The Roman army would soon crush Jerusalem and the Jews would be scattered outside of Palestine. Judgment would also come to those who put faith in themselves rather than in Christ.

When I think of the final Judgment Day, I…

27. Matthew 21:17-22

A SHRIVELED FIG TREE OBJECT LESSON

What life lessons have you had about faith?

2. Seeing the shriveled-up fig tree was an object lesson that Jesus used to energize the disciples' faith. What life experiences have energized your faith?

- ☐ I have seen answers to my prayers.
- ☐ I know people who have been healed by God.
- ☐ I have talked with missionaries who have told stories of God's power overseas.
- ☐ I have experienced God's healing.
- ☐ I have talked with friends or family about their answered prayers.
- ☐ I have heard sermons that have energized my faith.
- ☐ I have experienced God's presence in my life.

3. Jesus gives the illustration of moving mountains by faith not so his disciples could throw around mountain ranges, but so that they understood that the difficulties they face could be overcome through faith. Choose the top two difficulties young people can more easily face with faith in Christ.

- ☐ The death of a family member
- ☐ Career choices
- ☐ Lack of money
- ☐ Tough family situations
- ☐ Relationship problems with friends
- ☐ Homework hassles
- ☐ Depression and anxiety
- ☐ Dealing with teachers
- ☐ Sports stuff
- ☐ Saying no to temptation

4. The prayer promise applied to the disciples, but we can learn from this passage that God will hear our prayers. What are the top three things for which you pray the most?

#1 _____

#2 _____

#3 _____

5. Prayer has many benefits. (It is not the prayer that does something but the God to whom we pray.) A=agree, D=disagree, NC=no clue

- ___ Through prayer we can overcome life's difficulties.
- ___ Through prayer we can get any car we desire.
- ___ Through prayer we can find the courage to tell others of Christ's love.
- ___ Through prayer we can get an A on every test we take.
- ___ Through prayer we can ask for healing for ourselves and others.
- ___ Through prayer we can experience God's presence.
- ___ Through prayer we can grow closer to Christ.
- ___ Through prayer we can get a date for the prom.
- ___ Through prayer we can clarify God's direction for us.
- ___ Through prayer we can get rich.

READ OUT LOUD

After cleaning out the temple of salespeople, returning it at least temporarily to its mission of service to God, Jesus curses a fig tree to show judgment was coming soon. He didn't curse the tree out of anger or disappointment with its lack of fruit, but as an object lesson to the disciples of the coming judgment. Just as the tree was fruitless, so there are people who produce no spiritual fruit. Read this "difficult to understand" passage from Matthew 21:17-22.

ASK

Who, in your family, knows the most about faith?

DISCUSS, BY THE NUMBERS

1. The reality of Judgment Day is not often talked about. But the Bible tells us that those who choose to put their faith in themselves rather than Christ will one day be judged. Listen to your group members' completed sentences as you together talk about this reality.

2. Our life experiences can energize or weaken our faith in Christ. Like the disciples seeing the fig tree shrivel, your group members have experienced life lessons that have strengthened (or weakened) their faith. Talk about the meaning of these life lessons—how your group members have interpreted them in their lives.

3. Each of these situations can be faced with faith in Christ or through your own strength. Pick out several situations and talk about how with faith the situations are handled more easily. For example, the death of a family member is always devastating. But with faith, a Christian young person can rely on Christ to get through the grief one day at a time.

4. While shriveling up fig trees or moving mountains is not something we will do through prayer, God assures us that our prayers are heard. And God always responds with a "yes," "no," or "wait." Talk about the kinds of things for which your group

members pray. Discuss how they can expand the things for which they pray, from our elected officials to healing those who are sick in the congregation.

5. See commentary in bold after each statement.
   - Through prayer we can overcome life's difficulties. **Yes, as believers in Christ, we can with God's help**.
   - Through prayer we can get any car we desire. **No, we need to pray God's will.**
   - Through prayer we can find the courage to tell others of Christ's love. **Yes, because it is God's will for us to share the good news with others.**
   - Through prayer we can get an A on every test we take. **No, but we can pray that we will remember all that we studied.**
   - Through prayer we can ask for healing for others and ourselves. **Yes!**
   - Through prayer we can experience God's presence. **Yes!**
   - Through prayer we can grow closer to Christ. **Yes!**
   - Through prayer we can get a date for the prom. **Maybe.**
   - Through prayer we can clarify God's direction for us. **Yes!**
   - Through prayer we can get rich. **No, but we can get our daily bread.**

THE CLOSE

The disciples' faith was energized through the object lesson of the shriveled fig tree. Throughout their ministry with Christ, the experiences they went through with Jesus strengthened their faith. From seeing Christ feed thousands to watching him walking on water, their faith was energized. Our faith is also energized by life experiences. God takes us out of our comfort zone so that our faith in him is stretched. Instead of complaining about life, let's look at all the opportunities we have to increase and exercise our faith.

28. Mark 14:43-52

THE ARREST

How devoted are you to Jesus?

1. **Judas put his devotion to money over his devotion to Christ. When does money interfere with your relationship with Jesus?**

☐ When I don't need any money
☐ I don't think money gets in the way of my relationship with Christ
☐ When I envy others who do have money
☐ When I use money that I could give to God for things I don't really need
☐ When I feel like I can get money on my own
☐ When my friends who aren't Christians seem to have more money than I do
☐ When my prayers for things aren't answered the way I want

2. **Why do you think the religious leaders felt it necessary to send such a large mob of people with weapons to arrest Christ?**

a. They knew Jesus had mysterious powers.
b. They knew Jesus couldn't pull off any magic-trick miracle and get away with a crowd present.
c. They knew Jesus had a social phobia and didn't like to be around crowds.
d. They were hoping that the crowd would turn ugly, kill Jesus, and save them the trouble of having to put him on trial.
e. They thought that a couple of soldiers wouldn't be enough to handle the disciples if things turned ugly.
f. Judas had told them that they would need a crowd to take Jesus prisoner.

3. **Which of the following statements are true for you?**

___ Devotion to Christ brings joy to my life.
___ My devotion to Christ doesn't depend on what's happening to me.
___ Christ will punish me if my devotion to him wavers.
___ I want to remain devoted to all religions because you never know which one is correct.
___ My devotion to Christ demonstrates that I'm good enough to get into heaven.

4. **What do you think? Y (yes) or N (no)—**

___ Judas was a hypocrite.
___ The 11 disciples were hypocrites.
___ The religious leaders who wanted Jesus arrested were hypocrites.

___ The members of the mob sent to arrest Jesus were hypocrites.
___ Christians today are hypocrites.
___ Jesus was a hypocrite.

5. **Question Bombardment: Why do you think the disciples ran in fear from the mob sent to arrest Jesus? What situations prompt you to run from Christ? What encourages you to stay devoted to Christ?**

6. **How would you finish these sentences?**

—Jesus intentionally allowed himself to be arrested for me because . . .

—Christ intentionally suffered for me because . . .

—I should be intentionally devoted to Christ because . . .

7. **Isaiah 53 prophesied of Christ hundreds of years before his birth. What does Isaiah 53:3 say about your devotion to Christ?**

He was despised and rejected by others, a man of suffering, and familiar with pain. Like one from whom people hide their faces he was despised, and we held him in low esteem. (Isaiah 53:3)

READ OUT LOUD

Immediately before Jesus' arrest, he had been praying with the disciples—except for Judas, the treasurer of the group. Instead of being with Christ and the other disciples in prayer, Judas was off making a few extra bucks. His betrayal of Christ led to Jesus' arrest. Read the story from Mark 14:43-52.

ASK

How do you show your loyalty to your friends? To your family?

DISCUSS, BY THE NUMBERS

1. Get group consensus on the top two. Ask your group members to name one way they can keep money from interfering with their relationship with Christ. Money and possessions is one of the biggest roadblocks to devotion to Christ. Talk about what the group thinks devotion to Christ looks like. Devotion is an intentional commitment or loyalty to Christ.

2. We don't know for sure why a large mob was sent. Use this item to talk about how peer pressure (with young people or adults) can encourage or discourage devotion to Christ.

3. See commentary in bold after each statement.
    - Devotion to Christ brings joy to my life. **Joy is a by-product of our relationship with God—Romans 15:13; Galatians 5:22; Philippians 1:25; 1 Peter 1:8.**
    - My devotion to Christ doesn't depend on what's happening to me. **Joy comes from within. Happiness from external circumstances.**
    - Christ will punish me if my devotion to him wavers. **No, but we often think he might. We are preoccupied with what we must do to earn Christ's acceptance when it can't be earned.**
    - I want to remain devoted to all religions because you never know which one is correct. **Unfortunately, this is true for some who think all paths may lead to God.**

- My devotion to Christ demonstrates that I'm good enough to get into heaven. **Again, it is not about us but about what Christ, through the Holy Spirit, does in us and through us.**

4. This item demonstrates that everyone, except Jesus, is a hypocrite! Like Paul (Philippians 3:14), we strive to be more like Jesus but won't get there totally this side of heaven. Ask, "How can you more honestly walk your Christ-following talk?"

5. Talk through the questions together. Ask, "Why do you think Jesus stays devoted to us even though we are not always devoted to him?"

6. Listen to your group members' responses to the sentence stems. This item allows you to talk about Christ's willingness to go to the cross for us and our response to that.

7. It can be easy to philosophize about Isaiah 53:3 but tougher to personalize. Use this item to talk about how we need to regularly remind and encourage each other to be devoted to Christ. Our natural response is to reject Jesus.

THE CLOSE

The arrest of Jesus nudges us to consider our devotion to him. How devoted are we? How devoted do we want to be? Christ demonstrated his love for and devotion to us by going through the humiliation of the arrest and the bogus trial and enduring the punishment of the cross even though he was innocent. Don't we owe him our devotion?

JESUS BEFORE THE RELIGIOUS COURT

Looking for a reason to NOT believe in Christ

1. **What do you think are the chances of a person accused of a crime getting a fair trial today?**

   ☐ No chance
   ☐ Some chance
   ☐ A good chance
   ☐ A great chance

2. **Peter followed Christ from a distance. What do you think keeps people who are Christ-followers from getting closer to Jesus?** *(Check your top three.)*

   ☐ Fear
   ☐ Doubt
   ☐ Persecution
   ☐ Unbelieving family and friends
   ☐ Physical and emotional pain
   ☐ Greed
   ☐ Distractions by false teachings like *The Da Vinci Code* or Scientology

   ☐ The media making fun of Jesus
   ☐ A sin that is hard to let go of
   ☐ Self-help books that teach that you can do it on your own
   ☐ Scientific theories
   ☐ Other: _____

3. **The religious courtroom, held at Caiaphas' house, was filled with people willing to tell lies about Jesus. What lies do people tell about Jesus today?** *(Check the top two.)*

   ☐ Jesus is not God.
   ☐ Jesus faked his own death.
   ☐ Jesus did not come back to life.
   ☐ Jesus is part of the cosmic other.
   ☐ Jesus is a way to God.

   ☐ Jesus never existed.
   ☐ Jesus is boring.
   ☐ Jesus was a nice guy.
   ☐ Jesus was a prophet.
   ☐ Other: _____

4. **Why do you think some people so do not want to believe in Jesus as God who can save them from their sins?** *(Choose the top two.)*

   ☐ They don't believe they need the forgiveness that Jesus offers.
   ☐ They believe there are others ways to God than through Christ.
   ☐ They don't think much about spiritual things.
   ☐ They think that the answer to life is inside them.
   ☐ They think Christ is a crutch for weak people.
   ☐ They feel they are in control of their lives and don't need God.
   ☐ Other: _____

5. **Christ seems to refer to his return and final judgment as future proof that he is the promised Messiah. How often do you think of the final judgment? Is that the reason you should believe in Christ?**

READ OUT LOUD

After Jesus' arrest by the religious leaders, he stood trial before the Sanhedrin, the religious court of the Jews. The trial was bogus. Christ was quickly led to the home of the high priest, Caiaphas, who was the judge of the court. False witnesses were called to testify. Testimony was twisted to justify a quick conviction under the secrecy of darkness. The religious leaders were afraid of the authority of Jesus. His growing popularity was a threat to their rule and their power. Something had to be done, and done quickly. Read the story found in Mark 14:53-65.

ASK

Would you rather be a judge or a lawyer in a trial?

DISCUSS, BY THE NUMBERS

1. This item gets your group talking about trials and leads into a discussion of the unfair trial of Jesus.

2. See if there are a common three among your group members. Then talk about how easy it can be to follow Christ from a distance rather than totally commit. Ask, "What can we do as a group to help each other totally commit to Jesus?"

3. Go over each of the lies told about Jesus today. See what additional lies your group members have heard. Discuss how these lies twist the truth and deceive people, including some Christians.

4. The Sanhedrin didn't want to believe in Jesus even though they had all the evidence they needed to know that Jesus was the promised Messiah. Look at the reasons why people today don't think they need Jesus.

5. Use this item as a discussion starter to talk about the final judgment as a good or not-so-good reason to believe in Jesus as Savior.

THE CLOSE

There are some people today, just like during the time of Jesus, who want to find a reason to **not** believe in him. They put Jesus on trial and find him guilty of **not** being worth their time. What will you do with Jesus?

JESUS APPEARS BEFORE PILATE

Christ is full of surprises

1. **The religious leaders enjoyed the abusive treatment they gave Jesus. He was tied up like a common criminal. They liked the control they thought they had over Jesus. How do people try to control Jesus today?**
(Check the top two.)

- ☐ People try to be really good so that Jesus will give them what they want.
- ☐ People see Jesus as a genie in a bottle.
- ☐ People think Jesus is there for them as an easy way to avoid hell.
- ☐ People only talk to Jesus when they are in trouble.
- ☐ People believe only the parts of the Bible about Jesus that work for them.
- ☐ People give Jesus their problems along with the solutions they want.

2. **Jesus was brought before Pilate on trumped-up charges. What would you have said if Pilate had asked you to defend Jesus?**

3. **Pilate had to do something with Jesus. He couldn't let word get out that he let someone accused of treason off the hook or he would be in trouble with the ruling Caesar at the time, Emperor Tiberius. If word gets out that you think Jesus is your Lord and Savior, what would your friends think of you?**

4. **Jesus said nothing in response to the charges against him. Pilate was surprised. How surprised are you by what Jesus has done and is doing in your life?**

- ☐ Really surprised
- ☐ Somewhat surprised
- ☐ Not surprised at all
- ☐ Jesus hasn't done anything in my life

5. **Complete this sentence stem:**

    The thing that amazes me most about Jesus is—

READ OUT LOUD

Before bringing Jesus to Pilate (the secular ruler representing the Roman Empire), the Jewish religious court (the Sanhedrin) convicted Jesus of blasphemy—of saying he was equal to God. Yet, now before Pilate, they change the charge against Jesus. The Jewish leaders knew that Pilate would not listen to a religious conviction. He couldn't have cared less if Jesus said he were God or Superman. So the Sanhedrin trumped up a number of charges, the biggest being that of treason—of wanting to overthrow the Roman government (to be the King of the Jews). Read the story from Mark 15:1-5.

ASK

What surprised you most about middle school?

DISCUSS, BY THE NUMBERS

1. The religious leaders thought they had Jesus within their control. Oh, how we think we can control God! Talk about the strategies listed that people think will get Jesus to do what they want. Consider additional ones that your group members throw out. Talk about what it means to let Jesus take control of your life rather than try to control Jesus as the Sanhedrin attempted to do.

2. Listen to what your group members might say in defense of Jesus. The point is to consider why Christ was innocent of the trumped-up charge of treason—why he is who he said he was in New Testament times.

3. Pilate could not ignore the accusation of treason brought by the Sanhedrin. Word might get out that he was disloyal to the Roman Caesar, and that would be the end of life as Pilate knew it. Talk with the group about what life would be like if word got out that Jesus is their Lord and Savior.

4. Examine the surprise factor of your group members Use this as an opportunity to talk about how Jesus works in our lives—through other people, through the Bible, through life circumstances. Ask, "Are you praying that Jesus work in your life?"

5. Listen to the completed sentence stems and talk further about how Christ is full of wonderful surprises for those who follow him.

THE CLOSE

We serve a Jesus who is full of wonderful surprises. There is never a dull moment for those who commit their lives fully to following Jesus. Just as Pilate was surprised by how Christ acted, we will be surprised about how he works in our lives if we submit to him.

1. **Mary Magdalene woke early to head to the tomb, where she thought Jesus lay buried. She wanted to spend time with Jesus. In the box below, describe a time you spent with Jesus that was awesome.**

2. **Read these statements and decide whether they're T (true) or F (false) for you.**

___ I have had trouble, like the disciples, believing that Jesus came back from the dead (Mark 16:11).

___ Like Mary Magdalene, I am willing to reflect on what it meant for Jesus to hang dying on the cross for my sins (see Matthew 27:55-56).

___ I am a committed Christ-follower like Mary Magdalene (Mark 15:40).

___ Jesus has worked a miracle in my life, just as he did with Mary Magdalene (Mark 16:9).

___ I am convinced that my sins were crucified and buried with Christ (Galatians 2:20).

___ I am anxiously waiting for Christ to come back again (Hebrews 9:28).

3. **Mary Magdalene told two of the disciples about Jesus' disappearance from the tomb. Who are the two people you most often talk with about Jesus?**

1. _____

2. _____

Why do you think it is critical that you talk with these people often about Jesus?

4. **Which one of the following best describes your relationship with Christ?**

☐ **I am as excited as Mary Magdalene about my relationship with Christ.**

☐ **I am hopeful about my relationship with Jesus, wanting to run like Peter and John.**

☐ **I am more like the nine disciples who didn't run to see Jesus, a little down about my relationship with Christ.**

5. **Read 1 Corinthians 15:17 to yourself. Suppose Christ had not come back to life after dying on the cross that Friday afternoon. What would that mean to you?**

And if Christ has not been raised, your faith is futile; you are still in your sins. (1 Corinthians 15:17)

6. **Read Psalm 16:9-10 and compare it with Acts 2:25-32. Does this help you understand passages from the Old Testament that prophesy that Jesus was to rise from the dead?**

They still did not understand from Scripture that Jesus had to rise from the dead. (John 20:9)

READ OUT LOUD

It's Friday afternoon. Jesus is dead, an innocent man executed by the Roman government. Rushed to a borrowed tomb before Passover begins at sundown, he is quickly buried. Fast forward to Sunday morning—three days later according to the Jewish calendar—Jesus is alive. Read the story found in John 20:1-10.

ASK

What is worth running to learn about? Running to math class? Hurrying to worship? Getting to sports practice quickly?

DISCUSS, BY THE NUMBERS

1. Listen to the awesome times your group members have spent with Jesus. No or few examples? Then talk about what your group members can do to energize their time with Christ in prayer, Bible reading, reflection in silence, and other spiritual practices.
2. See commentary in bold after each statement.
    - I have had trouble, like the disciples, believing that Jesus came back from the dead (Mark 16:11). **It is important to wrestle with the truths of our Christian faith. Doubt does not mean a young person is abandoning his or her faith. Critical reflection can strengthen one's faith.**
    - Like Mary Magdalene, I am willing to reflect on what it meant for Jesus to hang dying on the cross for my sins (see Matthew 27:56). **Meditation on the suffering Christ did for us is healing (see Isaiah 53:5; 1 Peter 2:24).**
    - I am a committed Christ-follower like Mary Magdalene (Mark 15:40). **Without judging any of your group members' status as Christ-followers, talk about what it means to grow in faith as a follower of Christ.**
    - Jesus has worked a miracle in my life, just as he did with Mary Magdalene (Mark 16:9). **Let your group members share how Jesus is working in their lives.**
    - I am convinced that my sins were crucified and buried with Christ (Galatians 2:20). **Not always easy to understand, but from a heavenly perspective every believer has been crucified with Christ—their sins buried and gone.**
    - I am anxiously waiting for Christ to come back again (Hebrews 9:28). **Not something many Christians consider when reflecting on the empty tomb.**
3. Use this item to talk about the importance of faith conversations with other trustworthy Christians. We are to encourage one another (Romans 12:8; 1 Thessalonians 4:18) in the faith.
4. Excited; Hopeful; A Little Down. See which one of these best describes the relationship you and your group members have with Christ. Ask, "What keeps some people more excited about Christ than others?"
5. Read 1 Corinthians 15:17 out loud to your group. Then lead a dialogue about the necessity of the resurrection of Christ for Christianity to be valid. Ask, "How has your belief in the empty tomb changed your life?"

And if Christ has not been raised, your faith is futile; you are still in your sins. (1 Corinthians 15:17)

6. Read John 20:9. Make the point that the Old Testament did predict the death and resurrection of Christ but it was only after it happened that people understood these prophecies.

They still did not understand from Scripture that Jesus had to rise from the dead. (John 20:9)

THE CLOSE

The tomb was empty! The body was not moved. The death was not faked. Jesus is alive. And because of that fact, we are forgiven of our sins.

1. **Complete the sentence stem:**

   When Mary realized that Jesus was alive, she felt—

2. **Mary Magdalene was looking for Jesus. What do you think the average young person is looking for?** *(Check the top three.)*

32. John 20:11-18

MARY MAGDALENE LOOKS FOR THE LORD

What or whom are you looking for?

- ☐ a good time
- ☐ friends who really care
- ☐ a big bank account
- ☐ popularity
- ☐ inner peace
- ☐ highs from drugs/alcohol
- ☐ eternal life
- ☐ a right relationship with Allah
- ☐ revenge
- ☐ love
- ☐ a boyfriend or girlfriend
- ☐ meaning and purpose
- ☐ happiness
- ☐ sex
- ☐ freedom
- ☐ Jesus
- ☐ more stuff
- ☐ balance in their karma
- ☐ relief from emotional pain
- ☐ a good family life
- ☐ a better life
- ☐ a good education

3. **Go back to the list found in number 2 above. Place an ✖ in the box before the one thing that you are willing to do whatever it takes to have.**

4. **Mary, at first, didn't recognize Jesus. Maybe she was wrapped up in her grief; or perhaps she didn't expect to see him so failed to recognize him. When are you least likely to recognize Jesus involved in your life? When are you most likely?**

5. **When some of Jesus' followers left him, Christ asked his chosen Twelve if they too would abandon him. Peter speaks for the disciples when he says, in John 6:68-69, "Lord, to whom shall we go? You have the words of eternal life. We have come to believe and to know that you are the Holy One of God." What do you think is different about the words of Jesus and the words of other religions and philosophies of life?**

READ OUT LOUD
The empty tomb, at first, saddened Mary Magdalene. She came looking for Jesus, only to find, she thought, that his body had been moved. She desperately wanted to be with Jesus. And then, the unbelievable happened—Jesus was there with her—alive. Read the story found in John 20:11-18.

ASK
Where do you usually look first when you lose something important to you?

DISCUSS, BY THE NUMBERS
1. Listen to the completed sentence stems. Then, with your group, answer the questions that the sentence evoked.
2. Debate which are the top three; the point—to demonstrate that everyone, including young people, is looking for something.
3. You may get a Sunday school answer, but use this item to get serious in talking about what or whom your group is looking for. Is it really Jesus?
4. Talk about the fact that Jesus is always present in our lives. It is our awareness of his presence that fluctuates. Look for a pattern of when your group members are most aware and least aware of Christ's presence. Discuss how to raise our awareness of Christ's presence in our lives.
5. Use this question to talk about why Jesus does, in fact, have the words of life while other religions and philosophies may have a bit of the truth but leave us empty and searching for more.

THE CLOSE
Everyone is looking for something—fame, fortune, freedom, fun. *Something*. Our Christian faith teaches that, in Christ, we can find what's important in life—meaning and purpose, forgiveness, a relationship with God, eternal life. Many people look for these right things in the wrong places, such as false religions. Other people look for the wrong things in the wrong places, like alcohol or popularity. Have you found what you are looking for? You can, in Jesus Christ!

1. The religious leaders who conspired to put Jesus to death also tried to cover up the resurrection. Why do you think they wanted to cover up the truth?

2. The Roman soldiers who guarded the tomb were bribed with money to lie about the truth of Jesus. What do you think lures people away from the truth of the resurrection today?

- ❑ People don't want to be accountable to God for their sins, and, if the resurrection is true, they would then have to answer to God.
- ❑ Intellect and education can fool people into thinking they are wise enough not to believe in the resurrection of Jesus.
- ❑ People would rather not sacrifice their illusion of control over their lives. They don't want to make Jesus Lord because they like being lord.
- ❑ Materialism entices them into believing that this world is all there is—that there is no afterlife.
- ❑ People want to believe anything but the truth of the Bible.
- ❑ The busyness of today's world helps people avoid thinking about things like Jesus, sin, the resurrection, and eternal life.
- ❑ Satan lures people away from Jesus with the pleasures of this world.

3. Place an ✖ on the line indicating your opinion of Jesus.

■❑❑■

| Totally committed to Jesus | Going through the motions with Jesus | Anti-Jesus |

4. Why do you think some people are so openly hostile toward anything having to do with Jesus?

- ❑ They were hurt by Christians or Christianity as children.
- ❑ They are possessed by the devil.
- ❑ They are atheists.
- ❑ They see Jesus as a crutch.
- ❑ They have known Christians who have hurt them.
- ❑ They think Jesus is a threat to their religion.
- ❑ They think Jesus is for sissies.
- ❑ They think Christians are hypocrites.
- ❑ They believe Christians are arrogant because they believe Jesus is the only way.
- ❑ They get pleasure out of making fun of Christians.
- ❑ They have a lot of anger toward Christianity.
- ❑ They see themselves as smarter than Christians.

5. How do you know when someone is intentionally deceiving you about Jesus Christ?

Many deceivers, who do not acknowledge Jesus Christ as coming in the flesh, have gone out into the world. Any such person is the deceiver and the antichrist. (2 John 1:7)

6. What do you think?

- Mohammad, the founder of Islam, and Joseph Smith, the founder of Mormonism, both said they received God's word directly from God. But no witnesses were present to corroborate their stories. Why do you think people believe in Islam or Mormonism on the word of one person?
- L. Ron Hubbard created the religion of Scientology on a bet that he could invent a religion and people would follow it. Why would he knowingly deceive people? Why would people foolishly follow it?
- American New Age philosophies abound today. Here are some of their teachings:
  - *The truth is inside you.*
  - *You possess the innate wisdom to make the right decisions for your life.*
  - *Thinking it makes it so.*
- Why are these teachings false?

READ OUT LOUD

A contingent of Romans soldiers were ordered to guard the tomb of Jesus so that the body could not possibly have been stolen and a lie told about a resurrection. But the resurrection really happened. Bribes were paid. And a conspiracy began to hide the truth about Jesus. Read about this story from Matthew 27:62-66 and 28:11-15.

ASK

What is a conspiracy?

DISCUSS, BY THE NUMBERS

1. Here are some possible answers:
   - The religious leaders didn't want to believe in Jesus as their Savior.
   - Covering up the truth of the resurrection was easier than accepting Christ as the promised Messiah.
   - They were afraid of losing their money and power, which was more important to them than the truth.
   - Admitting that the resurrection of Jesus was true would mean that they were wrong.

Ask, "Are these same answers true today for those who don't want to believe in the resurrection of Christ?"

2. See commentary in bold after each statement.
   - People don't want to be accountable to God for their sins, and, if the resurrection is true, they would then have to answer to God. **People don't want to be reminded of their sinfulness. That's why New Age philosophies are so popular today—you don't have to look at the reality of sin because you are basically good.**
   - Intellect and education can fool people into thinking they are wise enough not to believe in the resurrection of Jesus. **College degrees are a wonderful thing. But sometimes people's brains and degrees get in the way of the truth instead of illuminating the truth.**
   - People would rather not sacrifice their illusion of control over their lives. They don't want to make Jesus Lord because they like being lord. **The human condition—the flesh, as the Bible calls it—wants to believe this illusion of control. "I am God," is what our sinfulness tells us. The truth there is a God, and you are not him, and thus not in control of the universe.**
   - Materialism entices them into believing that this world is all there is—that there is no afterlife. **Our abundance of stuff can fool us into forgetting about the spiritual world.**
   - People want to believe anything but the truth of the Bible. **And people will do all kinds of rationalizing to talk themselves out of believing the truth of the Bible.**
   - The busyness of today's world helps people avoid thinking about things like Jesus, sin, the resurrection, and eternal life. **One only has to stay busy for 70 or 80 years, not thinking about Jesus before it's too late.**
   - Satan lures people away from Jesus with the pleasures of this world. **This is true, but far too many times we blame the devil for our sinful choices. Satan may tempt, but we always have a choice.**

3. This item asks your group members to commit themselves to an opinion. Talk about what each of the three opinions assumes.
   - Totally committed to Jesus—100 percent onboard with my faith.
   - Going through the motions with Jesus—casual Christian.
   - Anti-Jesus—openly antagonistic toward anything having to do with Jesus.

4. This item helps you talk about why people can be so hostile to Jesus and the gospel. There are underlying causes. Understanding this can help your group members not be so afraid of those who are hostile.

5. We can know when someone is intentionally deceiving us about Jesus Christ because what they say contradicts Scripture. The Gnostics of the time of the apostle John taught that Jesus didn't exist in the flesh. John calls them deceivers and antichrists because they taught something contrary to Scripture.

Many deceivers, who do not acknowledge Jesus Christ as coming in the flesh, have gone out into the world. Any such person is the deceiver and the antichrist. (2 John 1:7)

6. Here are three scenarios in which lies are spread about spirituality. Talk about each as a way to discuss the deceptions that exist in today's world.

THE CLOSE

As politically incorrect as it may sound, Jesus is the only way, the only truth, and the only life, just as the Bible teaches. The exclusivity of Christianity has always been a problem for unbelievers. It is our human nature to believe that all paths lead to God—that there can't be only one way. We want to define a relationship with God on our terms. It has been said that the problem with Americans is not that they don't believe anything—but that they believe everything! The empty tomb and the subsequent cover-up of the resurrection prove one thing—that Jesus is the real deal.

JESUS & THE FISHING MIRACLE

Christ is there for us when we least expect him

1. Christ appeared to the disciples in a locked room on a Sunday while they contemplated his resurrection and (in this week's passage) during the week while they worked. Why do you think it is good to spend time with Christ on Sunday as well as during the week?

2. The seven disciples worked hard all night fishing yet caught nothing. They listened to Christ and caught more fish than they could imagine. What do you think Christ wanted them to learn from this object lesson?

   ❑ that he was there for them at a low point in their day
   ❑ that he was concerned about even the details of their lives
   ❑ that he was still in charge of the universe
   ❑ that he could do for the disciples what they couldn't do for themselves
   ❑ that he liked fishing
   ❑ that they were also to fish for the souls of people—a great reminder
   ❑ that he would meet their physical needs as well as their spiritual needs

3. John, Jesus' favorite disciple, was the first to recognize Jesus. How quickly do you experience Jesus' presence throughout your day?

   ❑ I often experience Christ's presence throughout my day.
   ❑ I sometimes experience Christ's presence throughout my day.
   ❑ I rarely or never experience Christ's presence throughout my day.

4. Peter, the most hyperactive and passionate of the disciples, couldn't wait to see Jesus. How excited are you to spend time with Jesus?

   a. I'm like Peter. I want to be the first to greet Jesus.
   b. I'm like John. I quickly recognize Jesus and want to be with him.
   c. I'm like the other five disciples. I know Jesus and want to spend time with him.
   d. Jesus hasn't appeared to me. I wouldn't recognize him.

5. Check five times from the following list when you most want Christ to be with you.

   ❑ While taking a math test
   ❑ When I'm out with my friends on Friday night
   ❑ At sports practice
   ❑ When I'm in trouble at home
   ❑ During worship at church
   ❑ When I'm reading my Bible
   ❑ While I'm flirting
   ❑ When I'm at work
   ❑ While I'm doing my homework
   ❑ While I'm doing my chores
   ❑ When I'm mad at my mom
   ❑ When a family friend dies

READ OUT LOUD

While Christ had appeared to individuals, he had appeared to the disciples twice—both times when the disciples were anxiously contemplating their next moves. In today's story, Jesus' third appearance, the disciples were waiting to meet Jesus at a predetermined spot on a mountain in Galilee (Matthew 28:16). They decided to go fishing, most likely because they needed the money. And then a miracle happened. Read the story found in John 21:1-14.

ASK

Who has surprised you by showing up at your home unexpectedly?

DISCUSS, BY THE NUMBERS

1. The disciples were together on Sunday after the resurrection locked in a room. Worshiping? Talking about faith? Singing hymns? Was this the first Sunday service? Suddenly Christ appears in their midst. In today's story, seven of the disciples were working during the week. Again, Christ appears. Too often today we leave Christ within the four walls of the church building. Use this item to talk about experiencing Christ's presence every day of the week.

2. Each of these statements could be true. Talk about each as you explore today's story further. Ask, "What do you think God has been teaching you this past week through the circumstances in your life?"

3. Each of the three answers is a valid answer. Encourage honest exploration rather than the Sunday school answer. Talk about how one experiences Christ's presence throughout an average day—through being sensitive to the voice of the Holy Spirit; through remembering Bible verses; through prayer; through listening to the circumstances of life; through friends; and more.

4. Listen to all the answers, including if "d" is given. Talk about how we each have a different relationship with Christ. Honestly talk about "d" since there may be some in your group who aren't Christians or who don't know what it means to experience Christ's presence.

5. This item explores the times your group members want Christ to be with them. Point out that Christ is with them always but that there are times when they don't sense his presence. Ask, "How has Jesus been there for you when you least expected him?"

THE CLOSE

Christ showed up when the disciples least expected him. And, to their surprise and delight, he performed a miracle that gave them both food to eat and fish to sell. Christ can show up in our lives when we least expect him as well. Actually, he is always with us, yet we don't always sense his presence. Christ wants to be with us. He longs to spend time with us. He is there for us no matter what.

1. **Peter denied Christ three times. Christ gives Peter three do-overs. Which of the following are true for you?**

- ☐ God has given me all kinds of do-overs or second chances.
- ☐ When God gives me a do-over, I learn from it and try not to need another one.
- ☐ I have abused God's second-chance policy.
- ☐ I judge others for getting do-overs but don't want others to judge me.
- ☐ God is too kind—he is willing to give me too many do-overs.
- ☐ I don't give people do-overs like God gives me.
- ☐ I will need more do-overs in the future.

2. **Why do you think God gives do-overs?**

3. **When Jesus told Peter, "When you are old you will stretch out your hands," he was referring to the fact that Peter would be crucified. Peter's do-over helped him become more committed to Christ. How do you think second chances help you become more committed to Christ?**

4. **In today's story Peter compared himself to John. How does your relationship with Christ compare to that of others?**

- ☐ I pray more than others
- ☐ I go to church more than others
- ☐ I read my Bible more than others
- ☐ I tell more people about Jesus
- ☐ I use God's name in vain more than others
- ☐ I gossip more than others
- ☐ I invite friends to church more than others
- ☐ I give more money to the Lord
- ☐ I dress more modestly
- ☐ I listen to the sermon more

- ☐ I pray less than others
- ☐ I go to church less than others
- ☐ I read my Bible less than others
- ☐ I tell fewer people about Jesus
- ☐ I use God's name in vain less than others
- ☐ I gossip less than others
- ☐ I invite friends to church less than others
- ☐ I give less money to the Lord
- ☐ I dress less modestly
- ☐ I listen to the sermon less

5. **Which one of the following statements best describes you?**

- ☐ What I have seen of Christ in the Bible is enough for me to believe.
- ☐ I don't know much about what the Bible says regarding Jesus.
- ☐ I'm still not convinced by what the Bible says that Jesus is God.

But these are written that you may believe that Jesus is the Messiah, the Son of God, and that by believing you may have life in his name. (John 20:31)

READ OUT LOUD

Peter denied Christ three times before the crucifixion, and, after the resurrection, Jesus gave him three chances to repair the hurt in their relationship. Read the story found in John 21:15-25.

ASK

In what sport should do-overs be allowed?

DISCUSS, BY THE NUMBERS

1. This item gives you a chance to explore the forgiveness that only Christ can give. Isn't grace amazing?

2. Take time to talk about grace—that God is in the business of forgiveness. We like to limit this grace by wagging our fingers as we talk about grace, by saying God forgives, but… or by attaching guilt to our talks about grace. Yet, God extends grace to those who have placed their trust in Jesus! Ask, "How should do-overs help you want to live differently?"

3. Church history teaches us that Peter was, in fact, crucified, and crucified upside-down (he didn't think he was worthy to die as Jesus did, with his head up). Explore the reasons how forgiveness of sin again and again and again is a reminder of God's grace and a great reason to live a holy life. Explore, with your group members, what positive steps they can take to increase their commitment to Jesus. Ask, "Do second chances help you get closer and more committed to Christ?"

4. It's natural for us to compare ourselves to others. Peter did it when he asked about how John would die after hearing his own fate. Comparing our faith to others' isn't always bad if it is done with the desire to strengthen our faith. However, if it is done out of envy and jealousy, it can only hurt us. Use this item to talk about why we are so much like Peter.

5. Ask, "Does the Bible give us sufficient information to decide what we will do with Jesus?"

THE CLOSE

God gives do-overs—second chances at getting it right, new opportunities to live a holy life for Jesus. Peter denied Christ three times before the crucifixion. And, without beating Peter up emotionally with guilt and shame, Jesus gives Peter a second chance—three do-overs, in fact—to get rid of the three denials forever. Are you looking for a do-over? Then Jesus is your kind of God.

1. **How could some of the 11 remaining disciples still doubt or fail to believe in Jesus 100 percent?** *(Choose your top one.)*

- ☐ They were being honest.
- ☐ They worshiped him yet had hesitations.
- ☐ They were slow to believe in the resurrection.
- ☐ They had sincere faith, yet they still had questions.
- ☐ They had a moment of wondering if the resurrection was really true.

36. Matthew 28:16-20

THE GREAT COMMISSION

Jesus gives us a project and a promise

2. **Finish this sentence:**

Knowing that Jesus is in charge of heaven and earth makes me want to—

All authority in heaven and on earth has been given to me.
—Jesus, in Matthew 28:18

3. **Jesus gave his disciples a job to do before he returned to heaven—to evangelize, baptize, and disciple. What do you think these three words mean?**

To *evangelize* means—

To *baptize* means—

To *disciple* means—

Therefore go and make disciples of all nations, baptizing them in the name of the Father and of the Son and of the Holy Spirit, and teaching them to obey everything I have commanded you.
—Jesus, in Matthew 28:19-20

4. **Check the following boxes if you've ever—**

- ☐ wondered if Christ was really with you.
- ☐ felt totally abandoned by Jesus.
- ☐ experienced Jesus working in and through you.
- ☐ felt the peace that only Jesus gives.
- ☐ seen Jesus answer your prayers.

And surely I am with you always, to the very end of the age.
—Jesus, in Matthew 28:20

5. **When Jesus was born, he was called Immanuel—which means "God with us" (Matthew 1:23). Before he departed this world, he again assured his followers that he is and always will be "God with us." How do you know that Jesus is "with you always"?**

READ OUT LOUD

Today's story covers the Great Commission, a recording of Christ's last words, which give both a job for us to do and a promise he will keep as we carry out that job. Read the story from Matthew 28:16-20.

ASK

Who do you most want to text after hearing a secret?

DISCUSS, BY THE NUMBERS

1. You can doubt and put your faith in Jesus at the same time. Doubt is an honest look at one's faith. Use this item to talk about healthy doubt, or doubt that gets us to further examine our faith. Ask, "How does knowing that some of the disciples doubted give you hope?"

2. Jesus began his Great Commission by reminding the 11 remaining disciples that he is all-powerful God. This must have given them courage to want to share the good news with the world. Listen to the completed sentences and then answer the questions that arose from doing this activity.

3. See if your group members can come up with their own definitions.
   - To *evangelize* means—to tell others the good news of Jesus Christ.
   - To *baptize* means—to give those who have been evangelized the symbol of water as an outward sign of the inward change that happens because of Christ.
   - To *disciple* means—to teach those who are evangelized and baptized what it means to follow Christ.

4. Read the words of Jesus from Matthew 28:20, found below. Then use this item to talk about what it means to have Jesus with us always.

   And surely I am with you always, to the very end of the age.—Jesus, in Matthew 28:20

5. This item helps you further explore Jesus' words in Matthew 28:20. If we have put our faith in Christ, then we can believe this promise. The longer we follow Christ, the more evidence we will have that this promise rings true.

THE CLOSE

A project and a promise—that's what Jesus gave us before he left. We have the privilege of sharing our Jesus story with the world. And we can be confident that Jesus will always be with us, no matter what happens to us, as we share this story.

1. The Sadducees didn't believe in Jesus' resurrection or the resurrection that was to occur in the last days. The preaching of Peter and John was a grave threat to everything that the Sadducees believed. Which of the following belief systems do you think is threatened the most by Christianity today?

- Mormonism—a mix of doctrines with mother and father gods, good works to earn your own planet, and baptism of the dead.
- Materialism—this is all there is, so get as much as you can.
- Islam—the Muslim religion, in which you have to earn your way to heaven.
- Atheism—there is no God.
- Judaism—waiting for the Messiah.
- Buddhism—achieve nirvana through meditation, study, and various other methods.
- Humanism—people are basically good; emphasis on people's abilities to find truth and decide what's moral.
- Hinduism—mix of religious traditions that adhere to such beliefs as karma, reincarnation, and a multiplicity of gods.

2. The disciples saw the number of Christians grow rapidly in Jerusalem. Today, the percentage of Christians is growing rapidly in Central and South America, Africa, and Asia. Why do you think Christianity is on the decline in the United States, Canada, and Europe?

3. Peter was filled with the Holy Spirit. This means that Peter (complete this sentence) —

4. Go back to item #1. Pick one of the belief systems. How does this belief system claim to provide salvation? How is it different than Christianity?

5. Peter and John, disciples of Jesus, talked about what they had seen Jesus do and heard Jesus say. It was impossible for them to deny the truth about Christ. What truth about Jesus do your friends hear from you?

- ☐ That Jesus is God.
- ☐ That Jesus died and rose from the dead.
- ☐ That Jesus can forgive them of their sins.
- ☐ That they can have a personal relationship with Jesus.
- ☐ That you have put your trust in Jesus.
- ☐ That there is a Jesus.
- ☐ Other: _____

As for us, we cannot help speaking about what we have seen and heard. (Acts 4:20)

READ OUT LOUD

Peter, in the name of Jesus, miraculously healed a beggar who was disabled since birth. He and John talked with the amazed crowd about what happened. Of course they gave the credit for the healing to Jesus. The religious leaders had the two of them arrested. Read the rest of the story from Acts 4:1-22.

ASK

Have you ever been so excited that you can't stop talking?

DISCUSS, BY THE NUMBERS

1. Use this item to talk about belief systems that compete with Christianity. The Sadducees saw emerging Christianity as a threat to their power and belief system. Today, the belief systems mentioned are competing with Christianity for people's attention. To deal with the competition, Christians are told to "tolerate" all other belief systems as equals. Many Christians, in learning to "appreciate" other belief systems, have been misled into thinking that "all paths lead to God."

2. There was no denying that a miracle healing had occurred. Jesus was the explanation for the healing. Ask, "Why do you think Americans want to deny the reality of Jesus today?" Use this item to explore Christianity's decline in the United States, Canada, and Europe and its rapid expansion in Central and South America, Africa, and Asia.

3. This means Peter was filled with the Holy Spirit. Talk about what your church believes about the role of the Holy Spirit.

4. Today's story is clear. Salvation is only possible through Jesus Christ. Talk about how Christianity is different than the "isms" mentioned—that Christianity is a relationship with Christ!

5. Peter and John were committed to telling others about the forgiveness and love available through Jesus Christ. Use this item to discuss strategies for sharing this good news with friends and relatives who have not put their faith in Christ.

THE CLOSE

The Sanhedrin, by rejecting Jesus, fulfilled the prophecy given in Psalm 118:22-23. Jesus, as Messiah and Savior, was difficult to deny. He fulfilled prophecy. Miracles were performed in his name. And that same Jesus is difficult to deny today. All kinds of good works are performed today in Jesus' name. He still works in the lives of millions of people. And he wants to work in our lives as well.

1. The Christ-followers in Jerusalem took church seriously. They believed in this community of faith—of looking out for each other. How well do the people in your congregation look out for each other? *(Place an X on the line below that best answers the question.)*

The people in our
congregation
look out for themselves

The people in our
congregation look
out for each other

38. Acts 4:32- 5:11

ANANIAS & SAPPHIRA WERE DEAD WRONG

We can live a life of integrity or hypocrisy

2. Finish this sentence:

The resurrection of Jesus was important to the apostles because—

3. The poor in Jerusalem were taken care of by the priests, who would let them eat the meat and grains that were brought as a sacrifice to God. But the priests shunned Christian Jews. So those Christians who had more than they needed provided for those Christians who didn't have enough. What's your opinion? **A=agree, D=disagree, DN=don't know**

___ Christians today who have more than they need should give to Christians who are poor.
___ Christians today don't trust God to take care of them like the apostles trusted God.
___ Placing your faith in Christ doesn't mean that God will take care of you.
___ If the church today tried to do what the church in Jerusalem did (sharing everything), it would be a disaster.
___ It's better to be a rich Christian than a poor Christian.
___ Taking care of the poor should be low on the priority list of the church.
___ Christians today should give what they can to their church without sacrificing any of their wants.

4. Which statements do you think are true and which do you think are false?

___ Ananias and Sapphira will be in heaven.
___ God needed to kill Ananias and Sapphira to set an example for the early church.
___ Ananias and Sapphira didn't have to sell their stuff.
___ God wants us to be honest with ourselves, each other, and him.
___ Ananias and Sapphira held back some of their money because they were afraid to trust in God's provision for them.

READ OUT LOUD

Ananias and Sapphira were part of the church in Jerusalem. This means that they most likely had put their faith in Jesus Christ. Yet, they seemed to have difficulty accepting that God would look out for them. They pledged to give all that they sold to the church to help poor Christians who had no resources, but they were dishonest with the church and with God. See what happens as a result of their hypocrisy by reading their story from Acts 4:32-5:11.

ASK

When was the last time you thought someone was a hypocrite?

DISCUSS, BY THE NUMBERS

1. Most congregations do a great job looking out for those in their midst who are hurting. But oftentimes a congregation's young people are unaware of all that is done for those in need—prayers for those with cancer, help with rent money, groceries for the unemployed. Use this opportunity to talk about (without using specific names) the needs that have been met through prayer, visitation, and financial help.

2. The resurrection of Jesus was, and still is, at the heart of the good news. Without the resurrection there is no forgiveness of sin. Talk about how we often forget about the resurrection except at Easter. The reason the apostles and other followers of Christ acted so boldly in spreading the gospel was because they witnessed Christ's resurrection. The miracles they performed proved to those who were not witnesses the reality of the resurrection.

3. The sharing of all that the Jerusalem Christians had in support of the poor provides a principle for us to follow today—Christians with much should share with Christians in need. Use these statements to talk about this principle taught in today's story.

4. It is often confusing to Christians today as to why God took the lives of Ananias and Sapphira. It seems harsh and unfair. But God had to establish early in church history that deception and hypocrisy could not be tolerated. The two believers did not have to sell their property or, once sold, give the money to the church. In holding back part of the money, they were dishonest with God. God wants us to be honest with ourselves, each other, and him. The death of Ananias and Sapphira served as an example for the early church. It serves as an example to us today as well. First, that the faith community called the church is an important community, and membership in it should be taken seriously. Second, the members of the church should take their commitments to each other and God seriously.

5. Two examples are given in today's story—one of integrity and another of hypocrisy. Find out where most of your group members feel they are. Talk about how we want to be in the middle, but God is calling us to a life of integrity. Remind your group members that God is a God of grace and mercy, and as they attempt to live a life of integrity, forgiveness is available.

THE CLOSE

The apostles witnessed with great power because they had seen Jesus come back from the dead. They had experienced the forgiveness of sin that only Jesus could legitimately offer. They lived out a life of integrity—walking their Christian talk. The example of Barnabas' integrity sits in stark contrast to the hypocrisy of Ananias and Sapphira. Today, Christ is asking us to make a choice of how we want to live.

1. Today's story begins by saying, "In those days when the number of disciples was increasing…" Why do you think the opposition that the church faced in Jerusalem contributed to its growth? Does opposition help or hurt the church today? How about your church?

2. A disagreement that broke out in the Jerusalem church was handled quickly. How do you think disagreements should be handled when they arise in your church?

   - Kick the people who are disagreeing out of our church.
   - Wait until the disagreement gets really bad before addressing it.
   - Give your pastor the job of telling those who disagree what to do.
   - Let the church board decide what to do.
   - Ask the leaders in your church to pray for a solution.
   - Ignore the disagreement and hope it goes away.
   - Our church never has disagreements.
   - Other: _____

3. **How would you handle this church disagreement?**

   a. Some in the congregation want to move the clock to the front of the worship center. Others want it to remain where it is in the back of the room. Another group wants the clock removed from the building. How would you handle this church disagreement?

   b. The college girl who is leading one of the high school small groups is living with her boyfriend. A parent gets mad and wants her removed from leadership. The small group members really like her and can't understand why she must leave. No one else has offered to lead the group. How would you handle this church disagreement?

   c. Three parents find out from their kids that the volunteer middle school leader was speeding with young people in the van. The leader gets mad at the young people for "squealing" and the young people get mad at their parents. How would you handle this church disagreement?

4. **How would you finish these?**

   The biggest disagreement in our church is…

   I can be part of the solution to this disagreement by…

5. **What's your opinion?**

   - I think I'm qualified and ready to be a leader in our church.
   - I think I'm qualified but not ready to be a leader in our church.
   - I don't think I'm qualified, nor am I ready to be a leader in our church.

READ OUT LOUD

In spite of opposition and persecution, the church in Jerusalem grew rapidly. And with the growth came problems. In today's story the apostles brought the members of the church together to solve a big problem that had arisen. Read the story from Acts 6:1-7.

ASK

Who in your family is the best problem solver?

DISCUSS, BY THE NUMBERS

1. Walk through each of the questions, remembering that there were times in church history in which opposition helped the church grow and times when opposition stifled growth.

2. Talk through each of the ideas for handling disagreements today in your congregation. Explore all options with your group. Remember that giving an immediate "right" answer will shut down discussion. And remember, the apostles didn't use their power to impose a solution but called the church together to discuss and then vote on people who would serve as the solution.

3. Talk through each of these three situations, asking, "How would you handle this church disagreement?" And don't let your group come up with some "pie in the sky" answer. Throw in a few twists and turns as they try to solve the problem to make it real life. Refer back to today's story for guidance when necessary.

4. Get practical here without gossiping or maligning the character of anyone in your congregation. Focus on solutions of which your group members can be a part.

5. The followers of Christ in Jerusalem came together and chose seven people to handle the problem that had arisen. But they didn't choose just anybody. The church chose people qualified to solve the problem. They chose men who were "known to be full of the Spirit and wisdom." Use this item to talk about the qualifications your group members think are necessary for leaders to solve the problems in your congregation.

THE CLOSE

Every church you ever attend will have problems. So too will any other group to which you belong. As members of the body of Christ, we have an obligation to help solve the problems and disagreements that arise. Like the apostles in today's story, we can pray for those who are trying to solve the problems. And we can contribute to the solution rather than being part of the problem.

1. **What do you like best? As a Christian, I want to be called—**

- Follower of the Way
- Jesus freak
- Christ-follower
- Born-againer
- Disciple
- Christian

SAUL MEETS JESUS

Jesus can turn anyone's life around

2. **If Jesus sent you a text message to get your attention to follow him more closely, what do you think it would say?**

3. **Jesus demonstrated that he wanted a personal relationship with Saul—speaking directly to him. On the line scale below, indicate with an X the kind of relationship you have with Christ.**

■□□□□□□□□□□□□□□□□□□□□□□□□□□□□□□□□□□■

Personal relationship   Antagonistic relationship
with Jesus Christ   with Jesus Christ

4. **Saul asked Jesus to identify himself. Who do most of your friends think Jesus is? (Choose your top two.)**

- ☐ A real killjoy
- ☐ A cosmic force
- ☐ Savior but not Lord
- ☐ Bible story character
- ☐ A prophet
- ☐ My friends don't think much about spiritual or religious things
- ☐ A great teacher
- ☐ Lord and Savior
- ☐ A good person
- ☐ A myth; he never existed
- ☐ An historical figure

5. **Saul went without eating or drinking most likely because he was overwhelmed by the guilt and shame of his sinfulness. His encounter with Jesus put him in touch with his brokenness. Have you ever been overwhelmed by your sinfulness?**

☐ Yes   ☐ A little   ☐ Not really

6. **Ananias seemed initially unwilling to see Saul, which would have been understandable given that Saul was viewed by Christians as an enemy of Christianity. When are you most unwilling to do what Christ asks you to do?**

Saul (who later becomes Paul), a persecutor of the early church, would today be convicted of murder. We first hear about this murderer at the stoning of Stephen (Acts 7:58). In today's story he is hunting down Christians. Let's look at Acts 9:1-19.

ASK

What usually has to happen to get people to turn their lives around?

DISCUSS, BY THE NUMBERS

1. In today's story those who initially followed Jesus were called "followers of the Way" or "those who belong to the Way." Ask the group to decide what they most want to be called and why. See commentary in bold.

   • *Follower of the Way*—**this term originated in the first century, before the term** *Christian* **was coined. It describes those who were followers of the ways of Jesus. Remember that Jesus said he was "the way" (John 14:6).**
   • *Jesus freak*—**this term originated in the 1960s to describe young people, mostly hippies, who followed Jesus.**
   • *Christ-follower*—**a term more recently in vogue as an alternative to the word "Christian."**
   • *Born-againer*—**a derogatory term used to make fun of Christians.**
   • *Disciple*—**a biblical term used to describe someone who followed and learned from Christ.**
   • *Christian*—**means "little Christ."**
2. Jesus got Saul's attention through a flash of light and a loud voice. Talk about the different messages your group members identified. Discuss how the Bible contains the essence of the messages written by your group members. Christ is trying to get our attention through the Bible. He also uses life crises, friends, parents, sermons, life stories or testimonies of others, music and more.

3. Not every church focuses on having a personal relationship with Christ. With that said, young people want that kind of God; a God who wants to know them intimately and wants to be known as a friend (see Christ's words in John 15:14). Talk with your group about what it means to have that kind of relationship.

4. Use this item to talk about each of the perspectives that people have regarding Christ. Focus on what it means to make Jesus both Savior and Lord. Ask, "What does one's life look like when Christ is both Savior and Lord?"

5. Once Saul got in touch with his brokenness, his sinfulness, he was able to allow Christ to take care of his sin problem. This turned his life around. It didn't matter what he had done in the past. Christ gave him a fresh start. And Christ can do the same for everyone—those who have committed all kinds of egregious sins and those who grew up with Jesus and don't feel they have a story of transformation to tell because they feel their sins aren't that bad.

6. Listen to the situations your group members describe. Talk about how even Ananias, who was talking with God through a vision, was initially unwilling to do what God asked. Brainstorm ways your group members can rely on the Lord more when asked to do something by Jesus.

THE CLOSE

Jesus is in the change business. He turned Saul's life around. He is turning your life around if you said you are sorry for your sins and invited him to take control of your life. Not matter how good or how bad you think you've been, unless you've been perfect, you need Jesus to direct your life.

1. **Finish this sentence:**

   When you believe that Jesus is God, you want to…

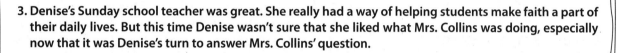

41. Acts 9:20-31

SAUL'S A CONVINCING CHRISTIAN

Convincing people that you love Jesus

2. **People were amazed by Saul's commitment to Christ. What do you think Christians could do today that would amaze people and demonstrate their commitment to Christ?**

3. **Denise's Sunday school teacher was great. She really had a way of helping students make faith a part of their daily lives. But this time Denise wasn't sure that she liked what Mrs. Collins was doing, especially now that it was Denise's turn to answer Mrs. Collins' question.**

   "Okay, Denise," said Mrs. Collins. "If you were in a country where being a Christian was illegal, what evidence would they have to convict you of your crime?"

   "Well," Denise began. Then she stopped. What could she be convicted of?

   "Well, I come to church," Denise said. Then she continued trying to convince the class that she could be guilty of being a Christian.

   How guilty are you of being a Christian? Describe the evidence.

4. **Give your opinion of the statements below—Yes, No, or Maybe.**

   a. My friends are convinced that I'm a Christian. _____
   b. At home, my family knows that I love Jesus. _____
   c. I play sports in a way that shows I'm a Christian. _____
   d. If you saw how I studied, you would say, "That person loves Jesus with all his heart, soul, and mind. _____
   e. When something bad happens to me, I react like I'm a believer in Jesus. _____

5. **Sometimes the book of Acts has been called the Acts of the Holy Spirit because the work of the Holy Spirit in the lives of Christians and the church is so prominent. How do you think the Holy Spirit is working in your church? In your life?**

   The church…was strengthened…and encouraged by the Holy Spirit… (Acts 9:31)

READ OUT LOUD

Saul, being transformed by Christ, was now convinced that Jesus is, in fact, God and the Savior of the world. He didn't waste time taking this revelation to others by preaching at every opportunity he could find. Read the story found in Acts 9:20-31.

ASK

Which of your teachers has tried to convince you of the importance of studying?

DISCUSS, BY THE NUMBERS

1. Saul was convinced that the Jesus he once hated was, in fact, the God of the universe and his Messiah. With this conviction, Saul made a clean break from his former life and embraced Christianity with all the fervor of someone convinced of its truth claims. Listen to the completed sentences of your group members as a great start to a discussion about being convinced and then convincing others of the reality of Jesus.

At once he began to preach in the synagogues that Jesus is the Son of God. (Acts 9:20)

2. Possible answers: Shun materialism and live a simpler life, giving their extra money to help the poor. Start programs to help the developmentally disabled. Serve the chronically mentally ill. Love the unlovable. Talk about what it means for Christians to walk the talk. Ask, "Would this amaze people who were not believers?"

*All those who heard [Saul] were astonished…
(Acts 9:21)*

3. Let your group members describe the evidence (or lack of) that could convict them of being a Christian. Discuss how we can easily become "Casual Christians" drifting away from a solid commitment to Christ.

4. This activity digs further into the evidence that exists of your Christianity. We need to be more like Saul and do a better job of convincing people in the different parts of our lives of our commitment to Christ.

Note: Statement "d" mentions mind *because Christ commands loving God with our minds (see Matthew 22:37). We can convince people of our commitment to Christ through our hard work in school!*

5. Use this item to talk about the big role the Holy Spirit played in the early church as well as the role the Holy Spirit plays in the life of the church today. Today, many young people are clueless about the Holy Spirit. Take this time to share the distinctive doctrinal teachings of your church.

The church…was strengthened…and encouraged by the Holy Spirit… (Acts 9:31)

THE CLOSE

Saul convincingly demonstrated that Jesus had turned his life around. As a new Christ-follower, Saul both showed and talked about his love for Jesus. Can we do the same? Can we show others through our attitudes and actions that we love Jesus? Can we talk often about our love for Jesus?

PAUL TELLS HIS FAITH STORY

What's your faith story?

1. **What do you like most about how Paul told his faith story (or his testimony) of what Jesus had done for him? What do you like the least?**

2. **Rate the following places according to where you would be most likely to share your faith story (i.e., testimony) with others by placing the letters of the following options by each item.**

   NW=No Way! CH=Could Happen, VL=Very Likely

   ___ in the school cafeteria
   ___ at my locker
   ___ on a date
   ___ at sports practice
   ___ on vacation
   ___ at work
   ___ in my neighborhood
   ___ at church
   ___ online
   ___ in a text message
   ___ other: _____

3. **Sharing your faith story is really nothing more than telling someone what Jesus Christ has meant to you and done for you. Paul did it, and so can you. Finish the sentences below to help yourself tell your story. Don't worry if you can't explain things very well or aren't sure what you believe. It's okay to have doubts and questions.**

   I believe that Jesus Christ—

   I believe that a true Christian is a person who—

   I first became aware of Jesus Christ when—

   I know that I am a Christian because—

   The best thing about being a Christian is—

4. **On the line scale below, indicate with an ✖ how scary it is for you to tell others your faith story.**

   ■□□■
   Scared to death   No worries. It's easy for me.

5. **Paul told his faith story in Aramaic, the language spoken by the Jews. He wanted them to clearly understand the good news about Jesus. What could you say to your friends who aren't believers in Christ that would make your message easy for them to understand?**

READ OUT LOUD

Paul, the apostle, courageously told his faith story (i.e., testimony) of what Jesus meant to him and had done for him. No matter where he was or who he was with, it seemed that Paul was always ready to talk Jesus with people. Read his faith story from Acts 21:37-22:21.

ASK

Who in your family tells the biggest "fish" story?

DISCUSS, BY THE NUMBERS

1. Here's a simple activity that can kick-start your conversation about faith stories/testimonies. Ask your group members to share what they liked most and least about Paul's approach to telling his story.

2. Like Paul, we need to be strategic as to where and when we share our faith stories. Talk about the need to be tactful without using this as an excuse not to share. Let your group members debate where and when is best for sharing their testimonies.

3. Use these sentence stems as the framework for a faith story/testimony. You may want your group members to practice sharing with each other. This helps them develop their stories further and gives them confidence to share with others.

4. This item gives you a chance to talk about the things that your group members fear most in telling others their faith stories. Share your fears as well and how you have (or have not) overcome them. Also, talk about why we share the good news of Jesus with others. It's not a game—one's broken relationship with God because of sin is serious. And our friends and relatives need the gospel. Without Christ they have no hope.

5. Listen to your group members' answers to the question, "What could you say to your friends who aren't believers in Christ that would make your message easy for them to understand?" Possible answers include: Share how you became a Christian; Jesus loves you no matter what you've done; I'll be bummed if you're not in heaven; putting your faith in Christ means your sins are forgiven.

THE CLOSE

Like Paul, we have many opportunities to tell others our faith story or testimony. Some who listen to us will put their faith in Christ, others will think about it and perhaps accept Christ and his message later, and still others will reject him. What will you do with your opportunities? Will you hide your faith, worried what others may think of you? Or will you boldly and strategically tell others your story? It's up to you!

1. **List five ways you think Christians are persecuted for their belief in Jesus Christ.**

    #1 _____

    #2 _____

    #3 _____

    #4 _____

    #5 _____

43. Acts 11:19-30

BARNABAS, THE ENCOURAGER

Let's encourage our Christian friends
to keep up the good work

2. **What are your Christian friends (peer & adult) doing right?**

   ☐ They are trying to become more like Jesus.
   ☐ They pray often.
   ☐ They read their Bibles regularly.
   ☐ They live the Golden Rule—they treat others the way they want to be treated.
   ☐ They fight for justice—for the poor, the disenfranchised, the homeless.
   ☐ They show mercy and compassion to others.
   ☐ They tell others about Jesus.
   ☐ They love their enemies.
   ☐ They forgive others as Christ has forgiven them.
   ☐ They live lives of integrity.
   ☐ They serve our community in the name of Jesus.
   ☐ Other: _____

3. **Barnabas' name meant "Son of Encouragement." He encouraged other Christians to continue the good work that Christ was doing in and through them. Here's your chance to be like Barnabas. Go back to item number 2. Circle the top two you want to encourage in the next week in your family and friends.**

4. **Barnabas went and found Paul (also named Saul) as a partner in encouraging other Christians. Together, as a team, they encouraged ("to give your courage to others") Christians to keep up the good work that they were doing. Who is another Christian that you could intentionally partner with to encourage others to live for Christ?**

5. **In what situations do you usually need the most encouragement? Who can be a Barnabas to you in these situations (name one adult and one young person)?**

6. **Christians from Antioch did a fundraiser for the hungry Christians from Jerusalem. What kind of fundraisers or other work does your group do for the hungry? Why do you think it is often Christians who feed the hungry, shelter those who are homeless, and visit those in prison?**

READ OUT LOUD

You would have wanted Barnabas to be on your side. His name says it all—it means "Son of Encouragement." The church in Jerusalem was in the midst of persecution by the Jewish religious leaders, who wanted nothing to do with Jesus. With the stoning of Stephen, Christians fled the city for new territory. It was God's way of fulfilling Acts 1:8. Barnabas offered all kinds of encouragement to those Christians who had moved out of Israel as well as to those who stayed. Read the story from Acts 11:19-30.

ASK

When do you usually need the most encouragement?

DISCUSS, BY THE NUMBERS

1. The result of the Jewish religious leaders' dispute with Christian Jews over Jesus led to persecution during the time of Barnabas. Today, persecution persists, but not as severely in the United States as in other countries. Answers might include things like being made fun of or cursed out to beatings, torture, and death. Talk about how fortunate we are to live in a country that protects religious freedom.

2. This item sets up a discussion of the need for encouragement (see item 3). Talk here about how many, many believers in Christ are more than just casual Christians—they are really trying to follow our Lord.

3. Tell your group that this is an opportunity to practice being like Barnabas. Go over the ideas your group members considered for encouraging their friends to live the Christian life.

4. Partnering with others in ministry can be key to ministry success, whether it is a ministry of encouragement such as Barnabas' or any other ministry. God didn't intend for us to go the Christian life alone.

5. Not only can your group members be like Barnabas, encouraging other Christians to keep up the good work they are doing for the Lord, but they can learn to receive encouragement as well. Discuss with your young people why they need both peers and adults in their lives as encouragers. They need peers because everyone needs people their age to give them a boost. They need adults because young people can benefit from the wisdom of older Christians who have life experiences that youth lack.

6. Explore what your congregation and youth ministry are doing in the way of ministry to the poor and hurting.

THE CLOSE

Christians in the days of Barnabas needed encouragement to keep the faith, to keep allowing Jesus to work through them, and to keep them going a day at a time. And Barnabas, the Son of Encouragement, was there for them. We are no different today. We need faith encouragement. To whom could you be a Barnabas? And who is a Barnabas to you?

1. Rank the following "witnessing" strategies from 1 (best) to 10 (worst).

_____ Wear a T-shirt with a Christian message.
_____ Tell people they are going to hell if they don't repent.
_____ Love your enemies.
_____ Develop friendships with those who don't know Christ.
_____ Place a bumper sticker on your car with a Christian message.
_____ Walk a non-Christian through the book of Romans.
_____ Use a pamphlet that gives the gospel message.
_____ Share what Christ has done for you.
_____ Invite non-Christian friends to your church.
_____ Act like a Christian when you're around those to whom you want to witness.

44. Acts 13:1-12
BARNABAS & PAUL SENT OUT AS MISSIONARIES
Getting out of your comfort zone to share the gospel

2. God wanted Paul and Barnabas to be missionaries (Christians who travel to another country or culture to share the good news of Jesus). If God wanted you to be a missionary, would you—

• Go for it?
• Think about it?
• Try to talk God into something else?
• Say, "No way"?

3. Name the missionaries your church supports with money and/or prayer.

4. Bar-Jesus, also known as Elymas, tried to block the gospel message told by Paul and Barnabas. Why do you think there are those who try to stop people from being interested in the good news about Jesus? A=agree, D=disagree

_____ They think it's fun.
_____ The devil controls them.
_____ They were hurt by church members when they were younger.
_____ They want to prove Christianity wrong.
_____ They're afraid to lose their friends.
_____ They believe religion is for weak-minded people.
_____ They want to hurt others.

5. Finish this sentence:

The ruler of the city, Sergius Paulus, was amazed by the message of Jesus because—

READ OUT LOUD

Barnabas had already gone out as a missionary. Then Paul (also known as Saul) and Barnabas were sent as missionaries to continue the work. Read the story found in Acts 13:1-12.

ASK

What country's name do you most want stamped on your passport?

DISCUSS, BY THE NUMBERS

1. See how close your group members were in their rankings. This will jumpstart a conversation on the best and worst ways to share the gospel. See if your group can create a top five list that would work best for them.
2. See where your group's comfort level is. Talk about the adventure of being a missionary. If your congregation promotes short-term mission opportunities, use this time to discuss the possibilities.
3. Ahead of time, get the names and locations, as well as the amount of money your congregation gives. Use this time to talk about the necessity of Christians going into other cultures to share the gospel, especially those cultures and nations that have no indigenous church from which the gospel can be spread.
4. Each of these statements describes a possible reason why some would attempt to block those interested in the good news about Jesus from hearing it. Talk about each statement. Ask your group to identify the top three. Then talk about how these could be overcome.
5. The miracle was proof that Jesus' message was true. This meant that Elymas was a fake and Jesus was for

real. Listen to the completed sentences and answer any questions that arise from the completions.

THE CLOSE

Barnabas and Paul were sent out as missionaries. They moved out of their comfort zones to do something great for God. For us, like them, we must move out of our comfort zones to share the gospel of Jesus with our family and friends.

1. **What's your opinion?** Like the people of Iconium, people today have all kinds of wild spiritual ideas because—

CONFUSION OVER WHAT TO BELIEVE

Compare what you hear to the truth found in Scripture

2. Paul and Barnabas shared the good news about Jesus' love and forgiveness with everyone they could. Even though some will reject him, why do you think everyone should be given the opportunity to learn about Jesus?

3. **The citizens of Lystra were convinced that there were many gods such as Zeus and Hermes. Why do you think people are so easily deceived (back then and today)?**

- ☐ They are idiots.
- ☐ Some people will believe anything.
- ☐ They want to be in charge of what is truth.
- ☐ They are desperate to latch on to some belief system.
- ☐ They don't know what they believe.
- ☐ They are easily influenced by whatever is new and sounds good.
- ☐ They are afraid.

4. **What do you think? Do you A (agree) or D (disagree)—**

___ Achieving high self-esteem is critical to living a productive life.
___ There's life on other planets with their own religions. How do we know? Who do you think helped build the pyramids—the aliens, of course.
___ It doesn't matter what you believe as long as you sincerely believe it.
___ If the good you do outweighs the bad, God lets you into heaven.
___ A psychic can't really contact the dead.
___ Astrology is a reliable way to tell if two people will be compatible.
___ There's scientific evidence that palm reading really works.
___ Reincarnation must be true since so many people in India believe in it.
___ You need only look inside to find god.

5. **How do you know what is truth and what is false teaching?**
(Place an ✖ on the line below that best answers the question.)

■☐☐☐☐☐☐☐☐☐☐☐☐☐☐☐☐☐☐☐☐☐☐☐☐☐☐☐☐☐☐☐☐☐☐☐☐☐☐☐■
I compare what I hear   I have absolutely no clue
to what the Bible says

6. **Paul and Barnabas showed their frustration over the crazy spiritual beliefs of the citizens of Lystra by tearing their clothes (a symbol for grief). What do you do when you get frustrated by wild, crazy beliefs that you hear from friends or see on TV?**

READ OUT LOUD

Confused over what to believe, the citizens of Iconium were divided by the preaching of Paul and Barnabas. While some believed in the gospel message, others reacted in anger and wanted nothing to do with the message or the messengers. In the city of Lystra, the two missionaries, Paul and Barnabas, had similar reactions. Read the story from Acts 14:1-15.

ASK

When do you know TV commercials are telling the truth? When do you know they are lying?

DISCUSS, BY THE NUMBERS

1. The citizens of Iconium were conflicted—some put their faith in Christ while others clung to their traditional gods. The wild spiritual ideas that people hold on to today are no different. In the face of the evidence, they reject the truth in favor of the most incredibly absurd ideas. Listen to your groups' completed sentences. This can start a fun discussion about the various crazy beliefs that are out there.

2. Paul and Barnabas patiently shared the gospel; but when the opposition became too great, they went elsewhere, continuing to share the gospel message with those who wanted to hear. Ask, "Have you ever felt like giving up telling others about Christ?"

3. Talk about how widespread spiritual deception has become, especially with New Age beliefs that "god" resides in each of us. Ask, "Why are so many Christians deceived? How can Christians avoid being deceived?"

4. See commentary in bold after each statement.
   - Achieving high self-esteem is critical to living a productive life. **The purpose of life is not to achieve a higher and higher self-image. In fact, you can feel too good about yourself—so good that you don't think you need God anymore. When you submit to Christ, you can have Christ-esteem, a realistic look at your brokenness and Christ's sufficiency.**
   - There is life on other planets with their own religions. How do we know? Who do you think helped build the pyramids—the aliens, of course. **Throughout the Bible, God focuses our attention on the need for salvation from sin through a Savior. There is no evidence in the Bible for extraterrestrial life, but finding it would not negate our need for Jesus.**
   - It doesn't matter what you believe as long as you sincerely believe it. **This is a variation of the "all paths lead to God" argument and contradicts the Bible, which says that Jesus is the way, the truth, and the life (John 14:6).**
   - If the good you do outweighs the bad, God lets you into heaven. **Good works have nothing to do with**

entrance into heaven. **The Scripture is clear that salvation can't be accomplished by our efforts, but only by what Christ has done (Ephesians 2:8).**

- A psychic can't really contact the dead. **The Bible clearly warns believers to avoid psychics (Leviticus 19:31, 20:6, 27; Deuteronomy 18:10–11; 1 Chronicles 10:13–14; Isaiah 8:19–20). There are all kinds of ways to fake contact with the dead, something that many psychics have mastered in order to take people's money.**

- Astrology is a reliable way to tell if two people will be compatible. **Neither Scripture nor scientific evidence supports studying the alignment of the planets and stars for this purpose. It's interesting, though, that most people know their astrological signs and many read their horoscopes in newspapers and online.**

- There's scientific evidence that palm reading really works. **No, as with psychics, palm reading is also faked.**

- Reincarnation must be true since so many people in India believe in it. **The number of believers has no correlation with the trustworthiness of a spiritual belief. The Bible says that you get one life and then judgment (Hebrews 9:27). The doctrine of reincarnation avoids dealing with the problem of sin because one gets many opportunities to become "good enough" to reach heaven.**

- You need only look inside to find god. **This is a New Age belief that says we are all connected to the universe—one with the One. Can't understand it? That's because it's not true!**

5. We must always compare truth claims to what the Bible says, as the Christians in Berea did (Acts 17:11). This means we must study the Scriptures to know what they say so we can make the comparison.

6. Use this item to talk about an appropriate reaction to the crazy beliefs that are so readily accepted today.

THE CLOSE

There seems to be no end to the numerous spiritual beliefs that Americans so readily accept as truth today. Even though the evidence for the veracity of Scripture and the gospel message has been established, people don't want to be accountable for their sins. And so they are open to whatever teaching sounds good to them and allows them to stay in control of their lives rather than submit to the authority of God. Christians need to be aware of the plethora of false teachings, comparing what they hear to what the Bible teaches. You won't ever be deceived if you are clear about what the Scripture teaches.

1. The Pharisees who had become followers of Christ wanted Christians who were not Jews to become Jewish Christians—to follow the Law of Moses. While we know that following the Old Testament Law can't save us, is it bad to follow the Ten Commandments (see Exodus 20:1-17)?

- ☐ Yes
- ☐ No
- ☐ I'm confused

2. Finish this sentence:

   Saved by grace means—

   …we believe it is through the grace of our Lord Jesus that we are saved… (Acts 15:11)

3. Instead of immediately telling those at the meeting how salvation by grace worked, Peter allowed the controversy to be debated for a long time. Why do you think it is good to talk through church controversies, giving everyone a chance to air their opinions?

4. The council that met at Jerusalem, after much debate, relied on the Bible (in this case, the Old Testament) and the teachings of Christ to settle the controversy over how a person is saved. So what exactly does the Bible teach about how one is saved?

- ☐ That you have to be baptized to be saved
- ☐ That your good works can save you
- ☐ That God does the saving—you can choose it or reject it
- ☐ That any religion will get you saved as long as you are sincere in your belief
- ☐ I wish I knew

5. What do you think—A (agree), D (disagree), or I (I have no idea)?

   ___ Christians don't have to keep the law because they are free in Christ.
   ___ If you can become a Christian by accepting God's free gift of salvation, then it's okay to keep on sinning.
   ___ If Christ died for the world, then everyone is saved no matter what they believe.
   ___ You can buy off God if you give enough money to the church.
   ___ Since we don't have to do anything to earn our salvation, then there is really no reason to serve the poor or help the hurting.
   ___ Because of God's grace and mercy, there must not be a hell.

READ OUT LOUD

Today's story describes one of the first big controversies that the church faced. Pharisees who had put their faith in Christ were hung up on their Jewish faith. They wanted to "Judaize" the non-Jews who were becoming Christians. "If you put your faith in Jesus," they said, "you also have to follow the Old Testament's laws." This led to confusion as to what it meant to be a Christian. A big meeting was held in Jerusalem, called in church history the Council at Jerusalem, to get some clarity. Read the story from Acts 15:1-21.

ASK

What clubs or sports teams are you a member of? What did you have to do to become a member?

DISCUSS, BY THE NUMBERS

1. It is clear from Scripture that the Old Testament Law was given to show us that we can't keep it perfectly to save ourselves—that we need a Savior. But that doesn't mean that the Ten Commandments are bad, just that we can't keep them. The Ten Commandments are a great way to live our lives. But they have nothing to do with our salvation.

2. Use this incomplete sentence to talk about grace, the undeserved kindness that God shows us in Christ that saves us. Some of the Jewish Christians were confused about grace, having grown up trying to keep the Old Testament Law. They wanted works (keeping the Law) plus grace to equal salvation. It was this Council of Jerusalem that clarified this confusion.

3. The Council of Jerusalem teaches us that healthy discussion can help to clarify church doctrinal confusion and controversy. Peter could have easily asserted his apostolic authority and squelched the discussion, but he didn't. While disputes over beliefs are inevitable in every church, lengthy and civil dialogue can help end them.

4. Serious Bible study is always critical in the midst of any controversy. How many times have you heard, "It says somewhere in the Bible that…" and then the speaker of those words goes on to say something not found in the Bible. Talk about each of the statements and decide whether or not it is found in the Bible. The only one clearly taught in Scripture is "that God does the saving—you can choose it or reject it."

5. See commentary in bold after each statement.
   - Christians don't have to keep the law because they are free in Christ.. **See Romans 3:20-24.**
   - If you can become a Christian by accepting God's free gift of salvation, then it's okay to keep on sinning. **No, Paul dispels this myth in Romans 6:1-2.**
   - If Christ died for the world, then everyone is saved no matter what they believe. **This is a belief called universalism but again Scripture doesn't teach this. For example, in John 3:16-18 Jesus tells us that we have a choice.**
   - You can buy off God if you give enough money to the church. **Wow, how many of us put money in the offering plate to appease God for another week? More common than you may think. But salvation and a relationship with God aren't about being bought off. It's about coming to God recognizing our brokenness and asking for forgiveness.**
   - Since we don't have to do anything to earn our salvation, then there is really no reason to serve the poor or help the hurting. **Salvation is free for the asking. But once we put our faith in Christ, we will want to live like Christ and serve others.**
   - Because of God's grace and mercy, there must not be a hell. **Christ taught us that there is a hell, but the Bible is less clear than people realize about this place. Most of what people know about hell is not from the Bible but from such books as Dante's *Inferno* and Milton's *Paradise Lost*.**

THE CLOSE

The Council at Jerusalem, the first of many church councils, clarified an early church controversy about salvation. They looked to the Bible and the teachings of Jesus for the answer. And the answer has been the same for the last 2,000 years—we are saved by grace through faith in Jesus Christ.

PAUL & SILAS THROWN IN JAIL

Trusting Christ no matter what the circumstances

1. **How do you think Paul and Silas were able to endure the horrific beatings and yet sing praise hymns to God while they were still in severe pain?**

   a. They were faking the praise. They really felt sorry for themselves.
   b. They knew that Christ was suffering with them.
   c. They had low blood sugar from not eating, which kept the focus off the pain.
   d. They were toughened up from working out twice a day.

2. **Prayer and praise helped Paul and Silas get through the agony of their beatings and jail time. How do you think prayer and praise could help you change your attitude? Y=yes, N=no**

   ___ Prayer and praise would put the focus on God instead of me.
   ___ God answers prayers immediately.
   ___ Prayer and praise would help me remember that God is in control.
   ___ God will change my attitude as I pray.
   ___ Reflecting on Christ through prayer and praise is a reminder of his presence with me.
   ___ Prayer and praise fakes your brain into feeling better.
   ___ No matter what your circumstances, prayer and praise demonstrates that you are trusting in God to get you through.

3. **Finish this sentence:**

   When my life circumstances stink, I can still trust Christ because…

4. **Why do you think the other prisoners stayed in their jail cells after the earthquake had opened the way to their freedom?**

   a. They realized there was something different about Paul and Silas, and they wanted to stick around and see what is was.
   b. They did not move because they were in shock.
   c. They were very well behaved prisoners.
   d. They were afraid they would be caught and beaten if they tried to escape.
   e. They were waiting for an encore because Paul and Silas were such good singers.
   f. Other: _____

5. **The jailor, after watching how Paul and Silas responded, wanted the relationship with Christ that they had. On the line scale below, indicate with an ✖ how well you are doing at showing others you are a follower of Christ.**

   ■□□■
   Perfect witness for Christ   Lousy witness for Christ

6. **In what situation have you found yourself that resembled Paul's and Silas' and tested your faith?**

READ OUT LOUD

Paul and Silas had gone to the city of Philippi, where they founded a new church. This is the same church to which, years later, Paul would write a letter that you get to read today. Their visit really paid off, even though they endured great pain while they were there. Read the story from Acts 16:16-40.

ASK

When is it easiest for you to trust someone?

DISCUSS, BY THE NUMBERS

1. Paul and Silas were able to reflect on the suffering Christ endured on the cross on their behalf, as well as knowing that Christ was present with them as they were beaten and recovering from the consequences of the whip. Ask, "What does it mean for us to identify with the suffering of Christ? How can the suffering Christ endured help us when we suffer?"

2. Use this item to talk about the importance of prayer and praise in our lives. Ask, "How do we get to a point where we can pray and praise no matter what is happening?" Point out that sometimes we need to "fake it until we make it," which means we need to pray and praise even when we don't feel like it. And eventually we will feel like it! Ask, "For what do you think Paul and Silas prayed?"

3. Listen to the completed sentences. Paul and Silas had experienced Christ's love and care for them such that they were now able to trust him no matter what happened to them. Answer questions that arise as a result of completing the sentence.

4. Use this item to talk about the influence Paul and Silas had on the prisoners who listened to their prayers and praise songs. Ask, "What kind of influence are we having for Christ on those around us?"

5. Create a large replication of the line scale on flip chart paper or a whiteboard.

   Ask each of your group members (including yourself) to place their X on the replicated line scale.

Then talk about what it means to be a witness for our Lord through our actions not our words.

6. Let your group members share their difficult-circumstance stories. Then talk about how a life lived by faith beats out one lived without faith.

THE CLOSE

Trusting Christ no matter the circumstances we face is easier said than done. Today's story reminds us that it is possible and that it is the best way to live. Imagine if Paul and Silas were not able to trust in Christ while in jail. They would have had a much tougher time. You see, life is difficult no matter whether you live it through faith or on your own power. And you will get through the tough times much better living by faith in Christ.

1. Paul lived like Jesus no matter where he was. Decide how you can live like Jesus no matter where you are.

	Always	Sometimes	Never
a. If you want to live like Jesus everywhere you go, then worship with other Christians must be a priority.	☐	☐	☐
b. Becoming more like Jesus must be something you think about.	☐	☐	☐
c. Spending time meditating and studying Scripture is key to living like Jesus.	☐	☐	☐
d. Hanging out with friends of faith will help you become more like Christ.	☐	☐	☐
e. Serving others is a critical part of living like Jesus.	☐	☐	☐

48. Acts 17:1-4, 10-12, 15-34; 18:1-6

PAUL GETS AROUND

Living like Jesus everywhere you go

2. Paul lived passionately for Christ because he knew that Jesus really did come back to life after suffering and dying on the cross. This passion was evident when he talked with others about Jesus. Complete this sentence:

I am passionate for Christ when—

3. The Berean believers didn't accept any new teaching without checking first with the Bible. How often do you check Scripture before believing some new fad, philosophy, or next new thing?

❑ **I always try to consider how what I hear compares with what the Bible teaches.**
❑ **I usually think about what the Bible says.**
❑ **I sometimes remember to compare what I hear with what the Bible says.**
❑ **I rarely consider biblical teaching.**
❑ **I never think about checking out what the Bible has to say.**

4. While in Athens Paul found out that the Athenians liked to talk about the next new thing. Here are some teachings you may hear on talk shows today. What do you think? A (agree) or D (disagree)—

___ **You can do what you want as long as it doesn't hurt anyone else.**
___ **Thinking it makes it so.**
___ **You can trust your higher self to guide you into happiness.**
___ **The goal of life is the pursuit of happiness.**
___ **People are basically good and want to do the right thing.**

___ **You have everything inside of you to live life well.**
___ **Jesus is one of many ways.**
___ **Reality comes from our own thinking.**
___ **We have innate wisdom that, once our minds are clear, can guide us.**
___ **Your feelings can be trusted to guide you in the right direction**

5. "You go to church?" Kevin asked in a surprised tone.

"Yes," said James. "Does that surprise you?"

"Not really," said Kevin. "I guess you just never talk about it."

"I've gone to church since before I can remember," James said. "I guess I don't even think about it because its something we just do in my family. I'd be glad to talk about it with you. You can even come with me to church this Sunday!"

"Whoa, James," said Kevin. "I wouldn't have asked if I thought you were going to get all religious. Give me a break."

Wow, James thought. *I actually talked to someone about my faith! So he really didn't want to hear about it now… but maybe I can do it again.*

What do you think of James' approach to talking God with Kevin?

READ OUT LOUD

Paul is on the move—first in Thessalonica, then Berea, on to Athens, and finally, Corinth. Everywhere he goes you see his passion for living like Jesus. He seems to want nothing more than for God to shape him so he looks more and more like Christ. Read of his travels from Acts 17:1-4, 10-12, 15-34, and 18:1-6.

ASK

Where is one place you've never been that you want to go?

DISCUSS, BY THE NUMBERS

1. Today's story begins with Paul in Thessalonica, worshiping in the synagogue, the Jewish meeting place. We see him hanging out with Christian friends like Silas. He talks often about Jesus. He prays, studies Scripture, and serves others. Paul, more than anything else, wants to be like Jesus. This activity offers five statements that are examples of being like Jesus. See which ones your group members check with an "Always" or a "Sometimes."

2. Listen to the completed sentences. Paul, knowing for a fact that Jesus rose from the dead and was telling the truth about God, lived with a passion to be more like Jesus wherever he went. Talk with your group about intentionally living with passion for Jesus Christ.

3. Too many times people today are misled and deceived into believing lies about how to live. From philosophy to psychology and medicine, it's easy to trick people into believing almost anything. If it's new it must be good, or so people think. But the Bible is the source of authority for living, and we need to check new teachings and belief systems against the Scriptures.

4. See commentary in bold after each statement.
   - You can do what you want as long as it doesn't hurt anyone else. **This relative morality makes almost anything ethical and can justify almost any action.**
   - Thinking it makes it so. **This belief means you create your own reality by what you think. So if you are poor, it's because you want to be poor.**
   - You can trust your higher self to guide you into happiness. **We were created in the image of God, but that image was damaged by sin. Life lived with "me" in control will be a disaster.**
   - The goal of life is the pursuit of happiness. **Despite what the Declaration of Independence says, the goal of the Christian life is to love God and neighbor—not the pursuit of happiness.**
   - You have everything inside of you to live life well. **Look deep inside and you will find only brokenness. We need Christ to live the good life.**
   - Jesus is one of many ways. **No, Jesus is THE WAY.**
   - Reality comes from our own thinking. **No, there's only one reality, and our thinking doesn't create it. Our thinking may give us a certain perspective on reality, but we don't create reality by thinking it.**
   - We are born with an innate wisdom that, once our mind is clear, can guide us. **The only innate wisdom we are born with is original sin, which, if we let that guide us, will only get us into trouble.**
   - People are basically good and want to do the right thing. **People are born broken and must submit to God to do what is right. Yes, people can do good things apart from God, but ultimately they are sinners in need of a Savior. On our own we are broken.**
   - Your feelings can be trusted to guide you in the right direction. **No, your feelings will take you all over the map. Right thinking can guide you. Feelings by themselves are neither good nor bad but can't be trusted as a reliable guide for one's life.**

5. Paul knew that he wasn't responsible for people converting to Christianity. He was only responsible for sharing his faith story with them. When the Jews became angry with him, he took the message of Christ to the Gentiles. We too are responsible for presenting the good news but not for conversions. Use this situation to talk about ways your group members can talk about God with their friends.

THE CLOSE

Paul was on the move for Christ. And everywhere he went you saw the evidence of a life lived for Jesus and like Jesus. His lifestyle is a model for us because he wanted nothing more than to please Christ. Nothing else mattered. His commitment to Christ can be our commitment. Let's pray that God continues to shape us to be more like Jesus.

1. You decide!

- Do you believe Paul presented enough information in order for his listeners to consider converting to Christianity? ☐ **Yes** ☐ **Maybe** ☐ **No**

- Which of the following listeners do you think converted?

  ☐ King Agrippa
  ☐ Agrippa's sister, Bernice
  ☐ Governor Festus
  ☐ High-ranking army officers
  ☐ Leading citizens
  ☐ The jail staff guarding Paul
  ☐ Jews who brought false charges against Paul

2. Why do you suppose Paul's listeners might have converted to Christianity?

☐ They wanted to turn from darkness to light.
☐ What they heard from Paul seemed to make sense.
☐ They were afraid to go to hell.
☐ They wanted what Paul had.
☐ They wanted the forgiveness from God Paul spoke about.
☐ They wanted a relationship with God.
☐ They were bored and this sounded like fun.
☐ They wanted to experience God's love.
☐ They knew they needed a Messiah.
☐ They knew that the Caesar wasn't God, and they wanted to live in the truth.

3. Paul shared his Jesus story (how he became a Christian—sometimes called a testimony or faith story) with the listeners in Governor Festus' meeting room. How well do you think Paul did?

☐ He knocked it out of the park.
☐ He confused them.
☐ He put them to sleep.

4. How is your Jesus story similar to Paul's?

☐ What Jesus story?
☐ Not even close.
☐ Paul and I think alike.
☐ I don't want to have a Jesus story like his; he got into trouble.
☐ I would like to have a Jesus story like Paul's.

5. Describe your Jesus story:

6. Finish this sentence:

I have told my Jesus story to—

READ OUT LOUD

For two years, Felix—the governor of Judea, who often brought Paul before him hoping to bribe the missionary—has unlawfully held Paul in prison. But Festus has become the new governor. Unsure of how to handle the delicate situation with Paul, a Roman citizen, he brings Paul before King Agrippa, another Roman ruler. (Read the rest of the story found in Acts 25:23-26:32.)

ASK

Who in your family keeps telling the same story over and over again?

DISCUSS, BY THE NUMBERS

1. Use this item to talk about the essentials one needs to share when telling others the gospel. Point out that there will always be some people who accept Jesus while others will reject him. Ask your group members to give reasons why they think some of Paul's listeners may have converted while others said no to Jesus and Christianity.

2. Use this item to discuss why people might become Christians today, including why your group members' friends might convert. Ask, "Should the reason why people convert shape how we present the gospel to them?"

3. Talk about Paul's presentation of the gospel—how good was it? Ask, "Why do you think Governor Festus thought Paul was out of his mind? Do you think it's crazy to become a Christian today?"

4. Use this item to explore how easy it is for your group members to share their Jesus story. Ask, "Do you have to have a dramatic story like Paul to share what Jesus has done for you?" Explore why it's often difficult to share the gospel—why it's so scary or embarrassing.

5. Use this time to have your group members practice sharing their Jesus story. First, share your story to show how easy it can be to share. Ask your group members to describe what Jesus has done for them (forgiven sin, given their lives purpose, shown unconditional love, etc.)

6. Use this item to help your group members identify people with whom they need to share their Jesus story. As an example to your group members, commit out loud to share your story with one person.

THE CLOSE

It's easier than you think to share your Jesus story—your faith story, your testimony—about what Jesus has done for you. Yet, we often make it more difficult than it needs to be. Telling others about Jesus is as easy as sharing what Jesus means to you.

1. The ship Paul was traveling in was falling apart due to the hurricane-strong winds. The sailors and passengers had lost all hope of survival. In what situations do you sometimes lose hope?

- ☐ When I'm not doing so well in school
- ☐ When I face a crisis with my friends
- ☐ When things seem to be falling apart with my family
- ☐ When I can't stop worrying
- ☐ When I get really moody
- ☐ When my anger gets out of control
- ☐ Other: _____

50. Acts 27:13-44

PAUL'S FAITH & A SHIPWRECK

Our faith can help us and others get through the storms of life

2. Paul advised the crew not to sail. He predicted a disastrous end to the voyage, yet his advice was ignored. What's the best advice you ever gave? What's the best advice you were ever given?

3. How do you think Paul's faith helped him in this stormy situation?

- ☐ His faith helped him a little.
- ☐ His faith gave him the confidence to know that he could rely on Christ no matter what the outcome of the storm.
- ☐ Faith doesn't help in real-life situations.
- ☐ Paul's faith wasn't strong enough to help him.
- ☐ Faith is a crutch for weak people who aren't strong enough to handle the storms of life.

4. Paul gained credibility with the crew because his prediction of disaster proved correct. How do you gain credibility with your friends and family so that they will listen to you about faith?

	Always	Sometimes	Never
a. I do the best job I possibly can in school.	☐	☐	☐
b. I always tell the truth.	☐	☐	☐
c. People know that I avoid gossip.	☐	☐	☐
d. People know that I can be trusted.	☐	☐	☐
e. I am respectful while on dates.	☐	☐	☐
f. People know I have strong values.	☐	☐	☐
g. People know that they can count on me when they are in trouble.	☐	☐	☐
h. I am a peacemaker.	☐	☐	☐
i. People would say that I am compassionate.	☐	☐	☐
j. I am hopeful around others.	☐	☐	☐

5. The Jewish leaders wanted Paul out of the way. Felix, the governor of Judea, held Paul illegally in prison for two years. The storm nearly killed Paul. And yet, Paul reached the safety of land. God looked out for Paul so that God's will would be accomplished. How do you think God is accomplishing his will in your life?

READ OUT LOUD

The apostle Paul is forced to undergo a treacherous trip to Rome to stand trial as a criminal before Emperor Nero, even though he was innocent of the charges. On the journey aboard a ship, Paul, along with the crew and passengers, is caught in a nasty storm. God uses Paul to save the lives of those onboard the ship. (Read the story found in Acts 27:13-44.)

ASK

What do you think is scarier to drive in—high winds or heavy rain?

DISCUSS, BY THE NUMBERS

1. Young and old alike face storms in life. Use this item to talk about some of those life difficulties. Let your young people share their "storm" stories. Don't criticize them for saying that they lost hope at some point. You can talk about the hope we have in Christ later in your discussion time.

2. Use this item to talk about both bad and good advice that your group members have given and been given. This can lead to a discussion later about how helping others is one example of what Christians are supposed to do. Just as Paul did in this story, Christians are to help others.

3. Each of these statements describes a way people look at faith. Good theology tells us that our faith gives us the confidence to know that we can rely on Christ no matter what happens. But there are many people who see it differently: Faith is for Sunday, Christians are weak, the Bible's full of fictional characters, etc. Ask, "How does your faith help you in the stormy situations you face?" "Is it better to develop your faith before the storms of life hit you or wait until they are beating you up?"

4. There are many more ways of gaining credibility with people than just the ones listed. Use this time to talk about how living a life of integrity shows we can be trusted in matters of faith. Though we all are hypocrites at times, it is necessary for us to walk our faith-talk if we are going to have credibility with the world.

5. God's will for us is sometimes sidetracked by our free will or life circumstances. But God continues to work to accomplish his will in the world. Talk about the barriers your group members may experience as God works in their lives—their personal sin, the sin of others, the work of the devil, temptations, and the like.

THE CLOSE

Everyone faces storms in life. Life is difficult at times whether you're a Christian or not. Yet, as people of faith in Christ we have an advantage when the storms of life knock us around. We have a Jesus who is there for us. We have a hope in Christ that can keep us going. We have the promises of Scripture that these difficulties won't last forever. Our faith can help us get through the storms of life. And we can then help others get through the storms they face.

1. **Why do you think some of Paul's Jewish listeners didn't put their faith in Christ?**

- ☐ They didn't want to give up what they already believed.
- ☐ They didn't want to repent of their sins.
- ☐ It sounded too easy.
- ☐ They didn't believe what he said.
- ☐ They thought they would get around to it later.
- ☐ They couldn't give up the belief that they had to work their way to heaven.
- ☐ They wanted to keep living the way they had been.

2. **The Jews in Rome had already heard about Jesus as the possible Messiah. How many of your friends who aren't Christians have heard about Jesus? How many of them would put their faith in Jesus if you talked more about your faith?**

3. **How often do you think of Christ during your day?**

- ☐ Often throughout my day
- ☐ A few times throughout my day
- ☐ Hardly ever during my day
- ☐ Never

4. **Finish this sentence:** If Jesus is to be first in my life, I will need to…

5. **What does it look like to put Jesus first in your life when you are—**

a. studying for a math test?

b. choosing friends?

c. picking a movie to see?

d. deciding what to do with your free time?

e. doing your chores?

f. buying clothes?

g. surfing the Internet?

6. **How many people do you think put their faith in Jesus during the two years Paul preached in Rome?**

- ☐ very few
- ☐ some
- ☐ plenty
- ☐ all of Rome

READ OUT LOUD

Paul is in Rome to stand trial before Emperor Nero on trumped-up charges from the Jewish leaders in Jerusalem. Nero hated Christians so much that he blamed them for the burning of Rome, something he himself allowed to happen. (Now read how Paul used his two-year Roman house arrest from Acts 28:17-31.)

ASK

How do you prioritize your classes in their order of importance?

DISCUSS, BY THE NUMBERS

1. After going over each of these reasons as well as adding additional ones, talk about how these same reasons keep your group members' friends from putting their faith in Christ.
2. Sharing one's faith like Paul requires that we talk often about Jesus. Yet, for most young people and adults this seems impossible. Use this time to discuss ideas about how this could become more routine.
3. This is one measure of the importance of Jesus in the lives of your group members. Talk about how to reflect on Jesus throughout the day—through Scripture, prayer, memories of what Christ has done, and the like.
4. Listen to the completed sentences. Talk about how your group members set the priorities in their lives.
5. See possible answers in bold.
   - a. studying for a math test? **Doing my best so that God is glorified through my intellect.**
   - b. choosing friends? **Finding good friends who have values that are aligned with mine so that they will support my godly decisions.**
   - c. picking a movie to go to? **Choosing a movie that I could watch with Jesus.**
   - d. deciding what to do with your free time? **Spending some of my free time communicating with Jesus.**
   - e. doing your chores? **Seeing my chores as service to God.**
   - f. buying clothes? **Choosing clothes that are modest.**
   - g. surfing the Internet? **Spending time on sites that are appropriate.**
6. Use this item to discuss who does the saving. God does the saving. It is our responsibility to share.

THE CLOSE

Paul was so comfortable talking with others about Jesus because he had made Jesus his number-one priority. We can do the same. Putting Jesus first in our lives means that we think about Jesus often. Putting Jesus first in our lives means we include Jesus in every decision we make. Putting Jesus first in our lives means that considering Jesus is routine.

QUESTIONS THE DISCIPLES ASKED JESUS

Never be afraid to ask faith questions

1. **Jesus called the Pharisees on their hypocrisy. The Pharisees' rules were those created by men and not God. Jesus was always clarifying what the Scriptures taught, which contradicted the teachings of the Pharisees.**

   When you sense that a belief contradicts what the Scripture teaches, you should—

   Then the disciples came to [Jesus] and asked, "Do you know that the Pharisees were offended when they heard this?" (Matthew 15:12)

2. **What do you think? Do you A (agree) or D (disagree) with these statements?**

   ___ We can be certain that Jesus will return again.
   ___ The unexpected return of Jesus should motivate us to live for him every day.
   ___ There's no way I'd be fooled about Christ's second coming.
   ___ Jesus will return in my lifetime.
   ___ People are too preoccupied with when Christ will return.

   As Jesus was sitting on the Mount of Olives, the disciples came to him privately. "Tell us," they said, "when will this happen, and what will be the sign of your coming and of the end of the age?" (Matthew 24:3)

3. **The disciples wanted to dig deeper into the meaning of Christ's teachings, so they asked questions. With whom have you had a faith conversation in the last month? How did this conversation strengthen your faith? What do you like most about faith conversations? How often do you have a faith conversation with one of your parents? What keeps you from having more faith conversations?**

   After [Jesus] had left the crowd and entered the house, his disciples asked him about this parable. (Mark 7:17)

4. **Jesus used this question to teach the disciples about humility, something they didn't expect to learn from their question.** Humility is key to living the Christian life.

   ☐ Always   ☐ Sometimes   ☐ Rarely   ☐ Never

   At that time the disciples came to Jesus and asked, "Who, then, is the greatest in the kingdom of heaven?" (Matthew 18:1)

5. **The disciples were often confused by what Jesus taught. Sometimes they asked him what he meant, but other times they were afraid. When you are confused by what Jesus taught or what other parts of the Bible mean, what should you do?**

   ☐ Hide it from others in my church, pretending instead that I know what the Bible says
   ☐ Ask someone I trust
   ☐ Avoid the topic
   ☐ Start attending another church
   ☐ Make up my own answer

   But they did not understand what [Jesus] meant and were afraid to ask him about it. (Mark 9:32)

READ OUT LOUD

The disciples often asked Jesus questions. We can learn from looking at the questions they asked. Five of those questions, found in the Gospels of Matthew, Mark, and Luke, are examined today.

ASK

Do you often ask great questions at school?

DISCUSS, BY THE NUMBERS

1. The truth is critical, yet when it comes to spiritual truth, the politically correct response is to hold all beliefs as equally valid. Encourage your group members to love the truth and question the truth claims of any belief that contradict what the Bible teaches.

2. See commentary in bold after each statement.
   - We can be certain that Jesus will return again. **Scripture clearly teaches that Christ will return, and we can count on it as much as we can count on his resurrection as being true.**
   - The unexpected return of Jesus should motivate us to live for him every day. **That's what the Bible teaches. A great passage on this can be found in 2 Peter 3:7-11.**
   - There is no way I would be fooled about Christ's second coming. **The theme of deception can be found throughout Matthew 24, where Jesus tells of his second coming. The disciples were curious about his return. Christ's answer of, "Watch out that no one deceives you," is as valid today as when Christ first said it nearly 2,000 years ago.**
   - Jesus will return in my lifetime. **No one knows but God the Father. It could be tomorrow or 100 years from now. And does it matter? What matters is how we live for Jesus today.**
   - People are too preoccupied with when Christ will return. **There is a preoccupation that is unhealthy if it takes our eyes off how we ought to live for Christ.**

3. Work through these questions as you discuss the importance of faith conversations with family, friends, and adults in your congregation.

4. Christ's answer most likely caught the disciples off guard. The greatest in the kingdom would not be asking this question. Humility is how Christ lived and how we are to live as followers of Christ. Our brokenness requires that we humbly obey God as we live each day for him.

5. Emphasize that it is okay to be confused about what Christ taught—about what the Bible teaches. No need to hide or avoid our confusion; instead just ask questions of people we trust in our congregation.

THE CLOSE

Faith questions promote our learning more about God and the Bible. Faith questions promote faith conversations that strengthen our faith. And faith questions help others overcome their shyness in asking their questions about the Bible, God, and faith. Don't be afraid to ask your questions because there is no such thing as a stupid faith question. Just ask the disciples.

50 creative discussions and provocative questions about what the Bible says concerning values and behavior, music videos, marriage, loneliness, Christian social action, and more.

High School TalkSheets—Updated!
50 Creative Discussions for High School Youth Groups

David Lynn
Retail $14.99
978-0-310-23852-2

youth
specialties

Add 50 more great questions to your library! These will get high schoolers discovering new perspectives on what the Bible says about the future, cheating, family life, problem solving, and so much more.

More High School TalkSheets—Updated!
50 More Creative Discussions for High School Youth Groups

David Lynn
Retail $16.99
978-0-310-23854-6

Visit www.youthspecialties.com or your local bookstore

youth
specialties

Jumpstart your junior high lessons with 50 provocative questions that launch your students into deep discussions on issues that matter such as loneliness, prayer, world hunger, wisdom, and much more.

Junior High and Middle School TalkSheets—Updated!
50 Creative Discussions for Junior High Youth Groups

David Lynn
Retail $14.99
978-0-310-23855-3

Visit www.youthspecialties.com or your local bookstore.

youth
specialties

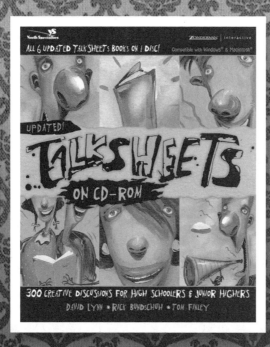

It's here, the CD-ROM you've been waiting for! Search all 300 Talk-Sheets discussion starters on dozens of relevant topics that resonate with students including friendship, family relationships, dating and marriage, addictions, social issues, faith, and more. You can search by topic, Bible reference, or keyword and customize the TalkSheets to fit your students' needs. Each TalkSheet includes a Bible study or two, activities, Internet resources, and provocative questions to start thought-provoking and focused conversations.

TalkSheets on CD-ROM
300 Creative Discussions for High Schoolers and Junior Highers

David Lynn, Rick Bundshuh, Tom Finley
Retail $69.99
978-0-310-25502-4

Visit www.youthspecialties.com or your local bookstore.